Dora eu directive

Made Simple

Willy DANENBERG

Published by Willy Danenenberg, 2026.

DORA EU DIRECTIVE

First edition. February 23, 2026.

ISBN: 979-8231613991

Written by Willy DANENBERG.

Table of Contents

DORA EU Directive Made Simple:

Building Digital Operational Resilience in Financial Services

Legal Notice

This book is intended for informational purposes only. While every effort has been made to ensure the accuracy of the information provided, the author and publisher assume no responsibility for errors, omissions, or damages resulting from the use of the information contained herein. The content does not constitute legal advice, and readers should consult qualified professionals for specific guidance regarding compliance with the Digital Operational Resilience Act (DORA) and related regulations.

Any references to organizations, products, or services are for illustrative purposes only and do not imply endorsement.

Sources Disclaimer

This book refers to EU directives, regulations, standards, and professional commentary. To support transparency and encourage further study, a curated list of the most important sources and citations is provided at the end of the book under *Links & NIS2 Sources & Relevance Table*

Trademarks

All trademarks, service marks, product names, and company names or logos mentioned in this book are the property of their respective owners. Use of these marks does not imply any affiliation, sponsorship, or endorsement.

ISBN

ISBN (Paperback):

ISBN 979-890030635-3

Praise for DORA EU Directive Made Simple

- "A must-read for any financial executive navigating the new DORA landscape. This guide turns complex regulatory jargon into practical, actionable insight."
- "In *DORA EU Directive Made Simple*, Willy Danenberg distills decades of experience into an engaging playbook for operational resilience. Both newcomers and seasoned professionals will find invaluable guidance here."
- "Comprehensive yet conversational, this book demystifies the Digital Operational Resilience Act. Danenberg's expertise shines through on every page."
- "Finally, a book that makes DORA approachable without losing its depth. Every chapter is a practical tool for building resilience."
- "Clear, authoritative, and highly relevant. This is the kind of resource that organizations will return to again and again."
- "Willy Danenberg has achieved the rare balance of insight and accessibility. A vital reference for anyone responsible for digital resilience."

In the Same Series

#	Title
1	DORA Made Simple
2	GDPR Made Simple
3	PCI DSS 4.0 Made Simple
4	NIS2 Made Simple
5	ISO 27001 Made Simple
6	PRINCE2 Made Simple
7	PMBOK Made Simple
8	Agile Made Simple
9	IT Architecture Made Simple
10	Scrum Made Simple
11	SAFe Made Simple
12	DR (Disaster Recovery) Made Simple
13	BCM (Business Continuity Management) Made Simple
14	EU AI Act Made Simple
15	AI for SaaS Made Simple
16	AI Ethics Made Simple
17	Generative AI Made Simple
18	AI Governance Made Simple

About the Author

Willy Danenberg is a senior consultant and expert in financial technology risk management with nearly 40 years of experience. Over his long career, he has advised numerous banks (including central banks and large multinational institutions) on strengthening their cybersecurity and operational resilience. Willy has been at the forefront of helping organizations adapt to evolving European regulations, from early banking IT guidelines to modern frameworks like DORA, GDPR, PCI DSS, ISO 27001 and NIS2. He is known for his practical, plain-language approach-breaking down complex regulatory requirements into clear strategies that organizations can implement. DORA EU Directive Made Simple is part of his mission to demystify compliance; it is part of a series of guides aimed at helping professionals understand and apply major EU regulations. When he's not consulting or writing, Willy speaks at industry conferences and mentors up-and-coming risk officers on building resilient, secure financial services.

Introduction

The Digital Operational Resilience Act (DORA) marks a new era in how financial institutions think about technology and risk. In today's world, banks and financial firms depend on complex IT systems and digital providers for almost every service. They are essentially *technology companies* as much as financial ones. This increased dependence on technology brings great benefits, but also significant vulnerabilities. Cyberattacks, IT outages, and system failures aren't just IT problems; they can disrupt critical banking services across borders and shake customer confidence.

A payment system going down or a data center failure at a cloud provider can have ripple effects on other companies and even the broader economy. Clearly, operational resilience-keeping services running in the face of shocks-has become just as important as traditional financial stability.

This is where DORA comes into play. Effective January 17, 2025, DORA is an EU regulation designed to ensure that banks, insurance companies, investment firms, and other financial entities can *withstand, respond to, and recover from* ICT (Information and Communication Technology) disruptions. ("Digital Operational Resilience Act (DORA) - EIOPA")

In essence, it's a comprehensive rulebook for digital operational resilience in the financial sector. Unlike prior guidelines that were often fragmented or advisory, DORA carries legal force across all EU member states (as a Regulation, it's a directly applicable law). It harmonizes how financial entities manage technology risks, report incidents, test their defenses, and oversee third-party IT providers. DORA isn't just about cybersecurity in the narrow sense of preventing hacks-it goes beyond cybersecurity to address operational continuity. It mandates that organizations plan for the worst, whether it's a cyberattack, hardware failure, or any IT glitch, so that essential financial services remain available come what may.

This book is your guide to understanding and implementing DORA in a *professional but conversational* tone. We will break down the regulation's requirements into plain English and practical steps. Whether you're an auditor, a consultant, a CEO of a bank, or an IT manager at a fintech startup, this book will help you grasp what DORA means for you and your organization. You'll learn not only what the law says, but why it matters and how you can comply in a smart, efficient way. We'll clarify technical terms as we go and provide real-world examples to illustrate key points. Think of it as having a friendly expert walk you through a complex new rule-by the end, DORA will feel much less daunting.

The structure of the book is as follows: Part 1 sets the stage, explaining why DORA represents a fundamental shift and how it fits into the broader regulatory ecosystem (alongside sister laws like NIS2 and GDPR). Part 2 dives into DORA's five core pillars-covering everything from risk management and incident reporting to testing, third-party risk, and information sharing. Part 3 is a hands-on roadmap from a consultant's perspective: how to assess your current resilience, plan a DORA compliance project, embed resilience into daily operations, prepare for audits, and communicate these efforts. Part 4 looks beyond the bare requirements-providing case studies, linking DORA to business continuity practices, warning of the consequences of inaction, and finally, showing how embracing DORA can become a competitive advantage. We'll conclude with final thoughts on building a resilient future.

By the end of this book, you should feel confident in understanding DORA's key mandates and equipped to take action. Compliance is not just a box-ticking exercise; it's an opportunity to strengthen your organization's backbone. So, let's get started on making DORA *simple*!

Part 1: The New Era of Financial Resilience

Part 1 introduces DORA and why it matters. We'll explore how this regulation came to be and why it's a game-changer for the financial sector's approach to technology risk. We'll identify who is affected by DORA, outline the new responsibilities it places on leadership, and see how regulators will enforce it. Crucially, we'll also position DORA in context with other major European laws like NIS2 (the new EU cybersecurity directive) and GDPR (data protection) to understand how they all fit together.

Chapter 1: The DORA Imperative - Beyond Cybersecurity

The DORA Imperative is simple: financial firms must elevate digital resilience to a top-tier priority, not just an IT issue. DORA's represents a fundamental shift in managing technology risk. In the past, banks and investment firms primarily focused on *cybersecurity* as preventing data breaches or hacks. DORA broadens that focus to operational resilience - ensuring critical functions continue even during tech disruptions. It's "beyond cybersecurity" because it's not only about keeping hackers out, but also about coping with any IT failure (malicious or not) without breaking the business.

Why was DORA needed? The financial sector's reliance on technology has skyrocketed and so have cyber threats. We've seen ransomware attacks freeze bank systems, IT outages ground payment processing, and third-party cloud incidents ripple across multiple companies. When a single tech incident can disrupt services across borders, it poses a systemic risk. For example, a simple software glitch at a stock exchange can halt trading in multiple countries, or a cyberattack on one bank can undermine trust in the whole sector. The EU recognized that existing rules were fragmented - some countries had guidelines, others not, and firms were following different standards. DORA is the EU's answer to create one harmonized framework that *every* financial entity must follow to manage ICT risk. It treats digital operational resilience as seriously as capital adequacy or liquidity in banking, moving it firmly into the boardroom.

DORA's approach is proactive rather than reactive. Instead of assuming incidents *might* happen, DORA assumes they will happen and demands firms prepare accordingly. This mindset shift echoes through all DORA's requirements - from conducting regular risk assessments and drills to having incident playbooks and backup systems ready to go. You'll appreciate that DORA isn't just another compliance burden; it's about fundamentally strengthening the trust and stability in our financial system. It's the difference between hoping nothing goes wrong and knowing you can handle it when it does.

Key terms used throughout DORA (and this book). For instance, DORA refers to ICT - Information and Communication Technology - which essentially means all your computers, networks, software, and digital services. Operational resilience means your ability to keep operating through difficulties. We'll encounter the concept of "critical or important functions" - these are the business activities that absolutely must stay running (for a bank, that might be payment transfers or online banking availability). Understanding these concepts sets the stage for the detailed requirements covered in later chapters. DORA's imperative is clear: prepare now, so that when disruption comes, you not only survive but continue to serve your customers.

Chapter 2: Who Must Comply?

DORA casts a wide net over the financial sector. We provide a clear guide to the scope of DORA, detailing which entities are subject to the regulation. If you're reading this to figure out "Does DORA apply to me?", this is your go-to section.

The regulation explicitly lists around 20 types of financial entities that must comply. These include the obvious players like banks (credit institutions) and insurance companies, but also a host of others: investment firms and asset managers, payment institutions and e-money institutions (think of your fintech payment apps and electronic money issuers), broker-dealers and trading venues (stock exchanges, etc.), central counterparties and central securities depositories (critical market infrastructure), credit rating agencies, and even crypto-asset service providers once they're authorized under the EU's crypto-assets regulations. In short, if it's a regulated financial service in the EU and relies on IT (which these days is virtually everyone), it's in scope. Traditional banks, online-only banks, insurance/reinsurance firms, pension funds, investment fund managers, payment processors, and even crowdfunding platforms - all must build digital operational resilience under DORA.

Importantly, ICT third-party service providers are also within DORA's scope. This means companies that supply tech services to financial entities - for example, cloud computing companies, core banking software vendors, data center operators, or fintech service providers - are indirectly affected. DORA imposes obligations on financial firms to manage risks from these providers and even creates an oversight framework for the *critical* ICT providers. So, big tech firms serving the finance industry will feel DORA's impact too.

Any notable exemptions or nuances in scope. For instance, very small institutions might enjoy simplified requirements in some cases, and certain categories like small investment firms or payment institutions might have proportionate treatment (DORA recognizes a one-size approach doesn't fit all - a tiny fintech vs. a global bank won't have the same resources). If you're a non-EU entity providing services into the EU, be aware: you could still be caught by DORA if you operate within the EU or serve EU clients in the covered sectors. Regulators will expect those activities to adhere to DORA standards as well.

If DORA applies to your organization, and for most readers of this book it likely will, you'll understand that your part of a broad community of entities all facing these requirements together.

Knowing who's in the same boat can be reassuring-you're not alone, and there will be industry-wide efforts and best practices emerging as everyone works toward compliance.

However, even if other entities that you may know of that are subject to DORA compliance do not comply fully, this does not free you from being compliant. Each entity will ultimately be judged for its compliance performance not necessarily relative to others or the sector.

Chapter 3: The Board's New Duty

One of DORA's most striking aspects is how it elevates digital resilience to a board-level responsibility or equivalent senior governing group of an organization. If you're a board member or C-level executive, DORA just added a new item to your job description.

Under DORA, the management body must define, approve, and oversee the digital operational resilience strategy. This is a big shift from the old mindset where cybersecurity or IT risk might have been delegated down to the IT department. Now, boards are explicitly accountable for ICT risk management. This is a huge change in corporate culture and organization. What does this entail? Firstly, the board needs to ensure that the firm has a comprehensive ICT Risk Management Framework. The board should approve this framework and periodically review it. It's expected to set the risk appetite - essentially, decide how much risk the organization is willing to tolerate when it comes to IT disruptions and cyber incidents - and ensure that resources are allocated to manage those risks.

In a way, GRC – Governance Risk and Compliance is not something anymore solely under the responsibility of a middle manager or a department head but is the responsibility of the highest authority in the company.

Ideally attached to the CEO, the COO or the board. In IT, often GRC was under the CSO but DORA may require that even the CSO comply meaning the GRC executive and team is systemic and is responsible and has oversight on all systems, departments and the interactions between all parties.

DORA also requires that board members stay informed about the evolving ICT risk landscape. A bank is not handling coins or bank notes much anymore but is a data management IT company for most of its operations.

Gone are the days when a bank board could claim ignorance of technology issues. Boards might need training on cyber risks or perhaps appoint members with expertise in digital resilience. Many institutions are already adding Chief Information Security Officers (CISOs) or technology risk reports to their board agendas.

Under DORA, this is not just best practice; it's mandatory that senior management actively participates in decisions like approving major IT investments, resilience testing plans, and incident response strategies.

An engaged board should do e.g., ask management tough questions about backup recovery times, insist on regular cyber drill exercises, and demand clear reporting on any major incidents or near-misses.

Also, both DORA and related laws like NIS2 make it clear that management can be held accountable (even personally) for serious oversights. While this doesn't mean a board director is expected to configure firewalls, it does mean regulators can sanction executives if they negligently ignore ICT risks.

This prospect of liability is meant to concentrate minds at the top. We provide tips for boards to fulfill their DORA duties: for example, establishing a board IT Risk Assessment Board (RAB), Change Request Advisory Board (CRAB) setting key performance indicators for operational resilience (like maximum allowable downtime for critical services), Rules to follow and review compliance with rules (including ideally rules as specific as additional rules per tool or system), and ensuring an incident response plan is not only on paper but practiced and updated with board involvement, approved checklists and more, Shareable Rule Books, great CMDB (Configuration management Data Base of IT hardware, software and also the data and the back up restore and data consistency reliability aspects of this..

In summary, digital resilience is now a governance issue. It encourages a culture where leadership doesn't see technology as a black box, but as an integral part of business strategy and risk management. The message to the boardroom is clear: treat digital operational resilience with the same seriousness as financial resilience and with urgency wherever a risk needs to be addressed. If you get this right at the top, the rest of the organization usually will follow.

Chapter 4: DORA and the Regulators

This chapter is all about how DORA will be supervised and enforced by authorities, and what financial organizations can expect from regulatory oversight. In other words, once you know *what* you need to do (from the earlier chapters), here we talk about *who* will check on you and *how*.

DORA involves a coordinated effort between national regulators and European-level authorities. Primarily, your familiar National Competent Authority (NCA) - such as your country's central bank or financial supervisory authority - will oversee your DORA compliance. If you're a bank in France, for example, the ACPR (French Prudential Supervision and Resolution Authority) will incorporate DORA requirements into its examinations. However, these national regulators aren't acting alone. The three European Supervisory Authorities (ESAs) - namely the EBA (European Banking Authority), ESMA (European Securities and Markets Authority), and EIOPA (European Insurance and Occupational Pensions Authority) - play a central coordinating role. ("European Supervisory Authorities publish joint warning on virtual ...") They will issue detailed guidance and Regulatory Technical Standards (RTS) to clarify how to implement DORA's requirements uniformly across Europe. Throughout this book, we might reference some RTS (for example, standards on incident classification or testing) - they are essentially rulebooks that flesh out DORA's high-level mandates with specifics.

What's unique in DORA is the oversight of critical ICT third-party service providers. If a tech provider (say a major cloud provider or core banking software company) is deemed *critical* for the financial sector, the EU can designate it as such. These critical providers will be subject to a Lead Overseer at the European level. Practically, this means a joint team led by one of the ESAs will directly monitor those tech firms - auditing their risk controls, demanding information, and even making recommendations or requests to address weaknesses. For financial entities, this means if you rely on a critical provider, you might see regulators scrutinizing that provider's resilience and your dependency on them. We will detail what you need to ensure in contracts with such providers, but here we note that regulators have new powers to *step in* and assess the tech providers themselves, not just the banks that use them. This is a novel approach: rather than only supervising banks about their vendors, authorities will also supervise the vendors about their service to banks.

Enforcement: DORA gives regulators teeth. National regulators can conduct inspections, request documentation of your resilience framework, and investigate incidents. If they find non-compliance, they can impose penalties. Fines can be significant, up to 2% of annual turnover for firms in breach. Regulators can also issue orders to fix problems, or in extreme cases, restrict a company's activities until issues are addressed. This chapter provides guidance on how to prepare for regulatory scrutiny: maintaining clear documentation, being transparent and proactive in communication with regulators, and treating regulatory inquiries not as adversarial but as a collaborative effort to improve resilience. Remember, regulators themselves are learning to implement DORA too, so early dialogue can help shape expectations.

By understanding the supervisory structure DORA sets up, you can better navigate compliance. Expect a mix of local and European oversight, surprise checks on both you and your critical suppliers, and the need to demonstrate not just *paper policies* but actual capability to respond to disruptions. Organizations that engage constructively with regulators (for example, participating in industry forums or feedback on draft technical standards) will likely fare better. The bottom line of Regulators are gearing up to enforce DORA rigorously, but if you know what they're looking for, you can turn examinations into an opportunity to showcase your firm's resilience posture.

Chapter 5: The DORA-NIS2-GDPR Ecosystem

The regulatory landscape can be alphabet soup, so in this crucial chapter we clarify how DORA interacts with two other major EU frameworks: NIS2 and GDPR.

Understanding overlaps and differences will help your organization create a unified compliance program rather than siloed efforts.

NIS2 is the EU's Second Network and Information Security Directive (Directive (EU) 2022/2555), a broad cybersecurity law covering many sectors (energy, transport, healthcare, finance, and more). If you're in the financial sector, technically both DORA and NIS2 could apply to you because finance is one of the critical sectors under NIS2. However, DORA is considered a lex specialis, the term "Lex Specialis" is Latin and translates to "special law" in English is derived from the legal maxim "lex specialis derogat legi generali", which means "a special law prevails over a general law."

For the financial sector under DORA, Lex Specialis means DORA takes precedence over NIS2 where there's overlap. In plain terms: for banks and other financial entities, DORA's rules on digital resilience generally override NIS2's more general cybersecurity requirements.

This avoids double jeopardy or conflicting duties. For example, both DORA and NIS2 require incident reporting, but if you're a bank, you will follow DORA's incident reporting mechanism as the primary route.

Important: Lex specialis doesn't mean NIS2 is completely irrelevant. DORA itself says that maintaining a strong relationship with the broader cyber framework is crucial. In areas not explicitly covered by DORA, NIS2 obligations still hold. So, if NIS2 has a requirement that DORA doesn't mention, a financial entity should comply with NIS2 too. An analogy: think of DORA as the specific rulebook for football, and NIS2 as the general rules for sports - if you're playing football, follow the football rulebook, but if something isn't addressed there, the general sports principles apply.

We'll highlight key differences: Scope - NIS2 covers a wide range of sectors and classifies entities as "essential" or "important" based on size/sector, whereas DORA laser-focuses on financial services.

Authority- NIS2 is enforced by national cybersecurity agencies (with no direct EU authority oversight), while DORA involves financial regulators and ESAs in a multi-layered oversight. Incident reporting deadlines - NIS2 tends to have very tight timelines (initial report within 24 hours of incident detection in many cases), whereas DORA requires prompt reporting "without undue delay" but with a bit more flexibility for detailed analysis in the reports. We provide a comparative table below to summarize these points.

Now, GDPR - the General Data Protection Regulation - is another pillar of EU compliance, focused on personal data protection and privacy. At first glance, GDPR (effective since 2018) and DORA (effective 2025) address different risks: GDPR cares about privacy (protecting personal data from misuse or breach), while DORA cares about operational continuity (keeping systems running and secure).

However, they do intersect. For example, a cyber incident at a bank might both disrupt services (triggering DORA's incident response) and leak customer data (triggering GDPR's personal data breach notification).

DORA explicitly does not override or replace GDPR. In fact, they are meant to complement each other. DORA shares the objective of safeguarding the confidentiality, integrity, and availability of data and systems-goals also central to GDPR's security principle. If you strengthen your ICT security under DORA, you're also reducing chances of a data breach under GDPR. But you must still follow GDPR's specific rules, like notifying data protection authorities within 72 hours of discovering a personal data breach and informing affected individuals if the breach is serious. From a compliance program perspective, this means your incident response plan should attain "two birds with one stone": one incident could require notifications to a financial regulator *and* a privacy regulator.

Another overlap: DORA requires keeping records of all ICT processes, assets, and third-party dependencies, and GDPR requires maintaining records of personal data processing (ROPA - Record of Processing Activities).

These can be aligned. When doing a DORA risk assessment, consider privacy risks too, and vice versa.

Also, under DORA's third-party risk rules, if a service provider handles personal data, you must have GDPR-compliant data processing agreements *in addition* to DORA's contractual terms. We'll cover strategies for integrating these efforts so you're not running two separate compliance projects.

In summary, ensure you see the big picture:

DORA is part of a trio of EU measures reinforcing each other. A financial entity in Europe must navigate all three - keeping systems resilient (DORA), keeping data safe (GDPR), and meeting broad cybersecurity standards (NIS2). It sounds daunting, but the good news is compliance efforts can be synergistic.

A strong cyber risk management framework will serve all three. Communication between your risk management team (DORA), your IT/security team (NIS2), and your data protection team (GDPR) is key.

We conclude the chapter with a comparison table to crystallize the main points:

Aspect	DORA (EU 2022/2554)	NIS2 (EU 2022/2555)	GDPR (EU 2016/679)
Focus/ Purpose	Financial sector **digital operational resilience** - ensure continuity of services under ICT disruptions. Covers ICT risk management, incident response, testing, third-party oversight.	Broad **cybersecurity** for essential/important entities in 18 sectors (energy, transport, health, **finance**, etc.) - improve overall network and information security.	**Data protection** and privacy - safeguard personal data, ensure lawful processing, and notify breaches.
Scope of Entities	~20 types of **financial entities** (banks, insurers, investment firms, payment and e-money institutions, crypto-asset providers, etc.) and their ICT service providers. Focused exclusively on finance.	**Critical and important entities** across many sectors (incl. finance). Finance sector entities are technically in scope, but DORA serves as lex specialis (sector-specific law) overriding NIS2 where applicable.	Virtually **all organizations** processing personal data of EU residents (across all sectors, large or small, if they handle personal data). Some SME exemptions, but banks/financial firms definitely in scope.
Legal Form	**Regulation** (directly applicable EU law). Uniform requirements across all Member States from day one (Jan 2025).	**Directive** - requires national transposition into laws. There may be slight variations country to country in implementation. NIS2 sets minimum standards to be met by 2024.	**Regulation** (direct EU law, in force since 2018). Uniform framework for data protection across EU; high-level principles require interpretation.
Primary Regulators	Financial regulators: National Competent Authorities (e.g., central banks, financial supervisory agencies) in coordination with European Supervisory Authorities (EBA, ESMA, EIOPA). ESAs also directly oversee *critical ICT third-party* providers.	National cybersecurity agencies or sectoral regulators. No direct EU central authority for NIS2; enforcement is by each Member State's appointed bodies (e.g., in Germany BSI for cyber, BaFin also for finance under NIS2).	National Data Protection Authorities (DPAs) in each country (e.g., CNIL in France, ICO in UK (pre-Brexit), etc.), coordinated by the European Data Protection Board (EDPB) for consistency.
Incident Reporting	**Major ICT incidents** must be reported "without undue delay" to financial regulator. DORA specifies a process: initial notification,	**Cyber incidents** must be reported quickly, often **within 24 hours** of detection for essential entities. Typically	**Personal data breaches** must be notified to DPAs within **72 hours** of becoming aware of the breach (if risk to individuals) and to

Aspect	DORA (EU 2022/2554)	NIS2 (EU 2022/2555)	GDPR (EU 2016/679)
	intermediate updates (if significant changes), and a final report after root-cause analysis. Clients must be informed if their financial interests are impacted. No fixed timeline in hours (allows flexibility for thorough reporting).	requires an initial report (24h), an intermediate report (within days), and final report (within one month) depending on severity (as per NIS2 guidance). Very tight, standardized reporting format across sectors.	affected individuals **without undue delay** if there's high risk. The focus is on breaches of personal data confidentiality/ integrity. Non-security incidents without data leakage don't trigger GDPR reports.
Penalties for Non-Compliance	Fines up to **2% of total annual worldwide turnover** for firms, and up to €1,000,000 for individuals (e.g., responsible managers)Critical ICT service providers face fines up to €5,000,000 or higher in some cases Additionally, regulators can impose remedial orders, public reprimands, or even ban companies from certain activities until issues are fixed.	Fines up to **€10 million or 2%** of global turnover (whichever higher) for essential entities; up to €7 million or 1.4% for important entities. Member States set exact fine regimes within those caps. Management liability is also highlighted-execs can be held accountable for negligence.	Fines up to **€20 million or 4%** of global turnover (whichever higher) for the most serious infringements (e.g., major data breaches or ignoring data subject rights). Lesser infringements up to 2% or €10M. DPAs can also impose corrective actions like suspension of data processing.

Table: High-level comparison of DORA, NIS2, and GDPR requirements and scope.

As you can see, DORA is tailored to financial services and integrates with financial supervision structures, while NIS2 is broader and GDPR is about data.

A bank, for instance, must satisfy all three: fortify IT systems (DORA/NIS2) and protect customer data (GDPR). Rather than viewing these as separate silos, smart organizations build a unified resilience and compliance program. For example, a single risk committee can oversee cyber risks for both DORA and NIS2 and involve the Data Protection Officer when personal data is involved. Incident response plans should have appendices for both DORA reporting and GDPR notification. Training programs for staff can cover both cybersecurity hygiene and data privacy best practices.

By aligning the goals of these regulations, you minimize duplication. Compliance efforts then serve multiple masters: an investment in encryption or backup systems, for instance, helps meet DORA's resilience goals, NIS2's security expectations, and GDPR's data protection mandate all at once. In the end, these regulations all drive towards a common vision - a Europe where digital services (especially in finance) are secure, reliable, and worthy of trust.

Part 2: The Five Pillars of DORA

Part 2 dives into the heart of DORA: its ***five key pillars****. Think of these pillars as the foundational components of digital operational resilience that every financial entity must build. Each chapter in this part explains one pillar in detail - what the requirements are, and how to fulfill them. By understanding all five pillars, you'll see the full picture of what DORA expects from organizations.*

Illustration: The five key pillars of DORA (Digital Operational Resilience Act) ensure that financial entities strengthen their ICT risk management, incident reporting, resilience testing, third-party risk management, and information sharing capabilities. By integrating these pillars into their operations, institutions can better withstand ICT disruptions, respond to incidents, and protect the stability of the financial system.

Chapter 6: Pillar 1 - ICT Risk Management Framework

We begin with the first and most foundational pillar: the ICT Risk Management Framework. Under DORA, every financial entity must establish **a comprehensive framework to manage Information and Communication Technology risks**. In simpler terms, this is the master plan for how you govern and handle all your technology-related risks, from cybersecurity threats to system downtimes.

What does this framework include? DORA outlines requirements covering governance, identification, protection, detection, response, and recovery - essentially the full lifecycle of risk management for ICT. Let's break that down:

- Governance: The management body needs to set the tone. The framework should clearly define roles and responsibilities for ICT risk. Who oversees what? For example, assign a Chief Information Security Officer (CISO) or Head of IT Risk, establish risk committees, and ensure the board oversees it. A strong governance structure means there is accountability, designated who does what and clarity and capability in decision-making for digital risks prevention and management.
- Risk Identification and Assessment: Firms must regularly identify their ICT risks. This means taking inventory of all critical business functions and the IT systems supporting them and then assessing what could go wrong. Threat modeling and risk assessment exercises are expected. Consider everything from cyber-attacks (like malware, phishing, insider threats) to technology failures (server crashes, telecom outages) to human errors. DORA pushes

organizations to move from being reactive to proactive in risk management Instead of waiting for an incident, regularly evaluate where you are vulnerable.

- Protection and Prevention: Once risks are identified, controls must be implemented to mitigate them. This includes technical measures (firewalls, access controls, encryption, up-to-date software patches) and organizational measures (policies, staff training, secure development practices). If, for instance, a risk is identified that a critical server could fail, a protection measure might be to build redundancy or backups for that server. DORA expects layered defenses to reduce the likelihood and impact of ICT incidents.
- Detection: Despite protections, incidents may happen, so you need to be able to detect them quickly. This involves monitoring systems, deploying intrusion detection tools, setting up alerts for unusual activities, etc. A key part of DORA compliance is having monitoring in place for networks and critical processes so that suspicious events are caught early. For example, if someone is trying to exfiltrate data or a system is suddenly using 100% CPU for unknown reasons, your team should get an alert.
- Response and Recovery: Even the best defenses can be breached, so DORA mandates robust incident response and business continuity planning (we'll go deeper into incident management in, and continuity later). The ICT risk framework must include documented incident response plans and recovery plans for various scenarios. How will you respond if a major incident occurs? The framework should spell out steps: isolate affected systems, communicate to stakeholders, invoke backup systems, etc. Similarly, recovery planning ensures you can restore operations - for example,

having data backups off-site and tested restoration procedures. DORA wants firms to not only put out fires but learn from them, so the framework should include post-incident review practices: analyzing root causes and updating controls so it doesn't happen again.

- ICT Risk Metrics and Monitoring: A good framework uses metrics to track how well you're managing risk. DORA doesn't prescribe specific metrics but expects regular reporting of risk indicators to management. This could be the number of high-severity incidents in a quarter, average time to recover systems (RTO - Recovery Time Objective performance), percentage of systems compliant with security patches, etc. These metrics help demonstrate to regulators (and yourself) that you have a handle and visibility on your risk posture.

In this chapter, we provided a step-by-step guide to creating or improving your ICT Risk Management Framework to meet DORA's standards. We included advice on developing risk assessment templates, creating an asset register (mapping business functions to IT systems and third-party providers as required), and ensuring alignment with international standards like ISO 27001 or the NIST framework, which can be helpful references. Wel also emphasize the need to document everything - policies, procedures, reports - because if a regulator asks, "Show me your risk management framework," you want to have a nice living, breathing binder (or intranet site) ready to show them.

DORA Pillar 1 is all about making ICT risk management a continuous, ingrained process in your organization and your organizational culture, structure and systemic. It's not a one-time project or a checkbox somewhere but is companywide obligation. It should be part of the development cycles, daily operations and decision-making. You should grasp that an effective ICT risk framework looks like and have a checklist of core components to implement, gates and tests to pass through and an overall IT architecture and process management architecture to match the required functions. Get this pillar right, and the rest of DORA becomes much easier, because you'll have a strong foundation to build upon.

Chapter 7: Pillar 2 - ICT-Related Incident Management

Despite best efforts in risk management (Pillar 1), incidents will happen. Pillar 2 of DORA focuses on how organizations must manage ICT-related incidents - especially the serious ones - when they occur. This chapter guides you through setting up a robust incident management and reporting framework, as required by DORA.

Incident Management under DORA starts with preparation: having internal processes to handle the detection, logging, and escalation of incidents. An *ICT-related incident* could be anything from a cyberattack (like a successful phishing that compromises accounts) to a hardware failure or even a data loss event.

DORA puts special emphasis on major incidents - those that severely disrupt services or have high impact on your operations or clients. One of the first tasks is to define what counts as a major incident for your organization.

Regulators (through the ESAs) have issued criteria for classification, usually based on factors like how many customers are affected, duration of downtime, financial loss, geographical spread, etc. In practice, you might categorize incidents into levels (Low, Medium, High) with clear thresholds (for example: "High severity if >25% of customers impacted or critical service outage > 1 hour"). We'll provide typical criteria and a template you can adapt.

Once an incident is identified, DORA mandates a structured reporting process. Here's what you need to do when a major incident strikes:

1. Initial Notification - Inform your national competent authority *without undue delay* once you determine an incident is major. DORA doesn't fix an exact hour count, but speed is of the essence (likely within the first day of

detection). The initial report is a short notification with basic facts: "We have incident X, detected at time Y, affecting service Z, we're investigating." Don't worry if you lack full details; the key is to put regulators on notice early.

2. Intermediate Updates - As the situation evolves, if there are significant developments (e.g., the incident spreads, or you discover the root cause, or the impact is larger than thought), you must send intermediate reports. These keep the authority in the loop. Think of it as "no surprises." If your systems remain down for an extended period, they should hear from you periodically rather than be left in the dark.
3. Final Report - Once the incident is resolved and you've done a root cause analysis, a detailed final report must be submitted to the regulator. This report will cover everything: what happened, why, how you handled it, what data or services were affected, what mitigation and recovery actions were taken, and importantly, lessons learned and measures to prevent recurrence. Regulators will scrutinize this, and it can't be a generic fluff document - it should demonstrate insight and concrete follow-up actions.

Additionally, DORA requires communication to clients or counterparts if the incident impacts them. For example, if a payment outage prevented customers from making transfers, you need to inform those customers in a timely manner (usually as soon as you're aware of it and can provide guidance). Transparent communication is part of resilience - it maintains trust. This chapter offers tips on incident communications: drafting customer notices or press statements and timing them appropriately.

We will also cover the internal incident response process: forming an incident response team, using playbooks for different scenarios (cyberattack vs. IT glitch), war / peace room coordination, and criteria for when to escalate to crisis management level.

Incorporating frameworks like NIST's incident response steps (Preparation, Detection & Analysis, Containment, Eradication, Recovery, Post-Incident) can be useful, and we map these to DORA requirements. A key point is documentation - keep records of all incidents and your handling of them, as auditors or regulators may ask to see evidence that you manage incidents systematically.

Finally, we explain how DORA's incident reporting dovetails with other laws (echoing Chapter 5): for instance, if the incident is a data breach, you have GDPR's 72-hour clock ticking for notifying DPAs; if it's also an operational outage that might fit NIS2's scope, you'd address that too. It might sound onerous to report to multiple regulators, but often you can draft one report and tailor it slightly for each audience. We provide an example scenario to illustrate say a cyberattack took down online banking and leaked data - you'd notify the financial regulator (DORA) and the privacy regulator (GDPR) with overlapping info.

In essence, Pillar 2 is about responding fast and effectively when trouble strikes and being transparent about it. By following DORA's incident management rules, organizations not only comply with the law but improve their crisis handling capability.

Many firms find that establishing these formal incident processes reduces chaos when the next incident happens - everyone knows their role and steps to take. As stressful as incidents are, DORA's framework ensures you don't face them unprepared or alone.

Chapter 8: Pillar 3: Digital Operational Resilience Testing and the TLPT Playbook

Testing is at the core of DORA's proactive approach. Chapter 8 delves into Pillar 3, which requires financial institutions to regularly test their digital operational resilience. The philosophy here is: *don't wait for a real incident to find out if your defenses work - test them in advance.* Through rigorous testing, you can discover weaknesses in your systems and processes and fix them before attackers (or Murphy's Law) exploit them.

DORA mandates a range of testing activities, from basic to advanced:

- Basic testing: This includes routine things like vulnerability scanning (automated tools scanning your network for known security holes), software code reviews, penetration testing (ethical hacking exercises) on a smaller scale, testing of data backups and restore procedures, etc. Many organizations already do these as part of good IT practice, but DORA formalizes it. You need to have a plan to cover all critical ICT systems with appropriate tests periodically. For example, ensure that every critical application undergoes at least an annual penetration test and that all critical data backups are tested for restorability.
- Advanced testing: For larger or more significant entities, DORA introduces Threat-Led Penetration Testing (TLPT), which we will cover in depth later. TLPT is like a "full dress rehearsal" of how your organization stands up to a real-world cyberattack, complete with professional red-team hackers trying to breach you using tactics mimicking real threats.

This chapter provides a step-by-step guide to building a resilience testing program. First, you need to develop a testing policy - a document that outlines what types of tests you conduct, frequency, scope, and how you'll track issues found. Regulators will expect to see that you have a systematic testing schedule covering all five pillars. For example, you might schedule quarterly vulnerability scans, annual disaster recovery exercises, a biennial crisis management simulation, and so on.

We emphasize the importance of testing not just technical defenses, but also procedures and people and communication. Table-top exercises (simulated scenario discussions) can test if your incident response plan works. Gather your IT staff, business continuity team, and executives in a room, present a hypothetical scenario ("ransomware has hit our trading system - go!") and see how they respond. These drills often reveal gaps (maybe two departments thought the other would inform customers, or maybe your backup didn't cover a particular system). DORA encourages these holistic tests to ensure *operational* resilience, not only IT security.

Another key aspect is cyber range or war-gaming exercises where possible, especially for big institutions.

A famous industry-wide exercise (like the European Central Bank's TLPT exercises under the TIBER-EU framework) to illustrate how realistic simulations are done can be used and provide very usefull insights.

While smaller firms won't have massive war rooms, they can still simulate scenarios at an appropriate scale.

The governance of testing: who authorizes tests (especially dangerous ones like live penetration tests on production systems), how to ensure safety (you don't want to accidentally cause outages during testing), and how to handle findings. It's critical that test results feed into improvements - DORA will expect you to fix the vulnerabilities and issues identified.

Regulators might ask: "When was the last resilience test and what did you learn from it? Show us the remediation actions."

A practical highlight in this chapter is a list of various types of tests and what they achieve:

- *Backup Restoration Test:* verifies you can restore data from backups (addresses resilience in case of data loss).
- *Disaster Recovery (DR) Exercise:* tests switching over to backup systems or secondary sites (addresses continuity if primary IT fails).
- *Cyber Penetration Test:* identifies security vulnerabilities an attacker could exploit (addresses protection and detection).
- *Emergency Communication Drill:* tests that your call trees and notification systems work (addresses incident response communication).
- *Tabletop Exercise:* tests decision-making and roles during a crisis (addresses governance and response coordination).

Testing isn't a one-off annual penetration test to satisfy an audit. It's an ongoing cycle of continuous improvement: test, find gaps, fix gaps, repeat.

The goal is to build confidence that, as threats evolve and systems change, your resilience keeps pace. DORA effectively forces organizations to adopt a mindset of "always be testing" because that's the only way to ensure everything will work when needed. And remember, testing under DORA is not about pass/fail grades - it's about learning and strengthening continuous improvements and RCA's Root Cause Analysis. Even a test that "fails" (like a DR test where not all systems recovered) is valuable if you use it to bolster your plan.

In summary, Pillar 3 ensures that firms don't just assume they're resilient - they prove it to themselves through regular drills and checks. That way, there are fewer nasty surprises when real incidents occur.

The TLPT Playbook

This is a hands-on guide to one of DORA's most demanding requirements for significant institutions: Threat-Led Penetration Testing (TLPT).

Consider this the playbook for how to prepare for and execute a TLPT, which is essentially a high-level, regulator-mandated "red team" exercise.

What is TLPT? It's an advanced form of penetration testing where a team of ethical hackers (the "red team") is given permission to simulate an attack on your organization, using tactics and techniques that real threat actors (like cybercriminal gangs or nation-state hackers) would use. It's "threat-led" because it starts with threat intelligence - understanding who might attack you and how - and then replicates those methods to see if you can withstand them.

A crucial element is that your defenders (the IT security team, the "blue team") usually are *not told in advance* that it's a test. They will perceive it as a real attack, which allows an authentic evaluation of your detection and response capabilities. Only a small, trusted group (called the White Team or Control Team) inside the organization knows about the test to ensure safety and to stop the test if needed.

Under DORA, TLPT is required at least every three years for certain entities. Typically, this will apply to larger institutions like big banks, or any firm deemed significant (the exact criteria are set in regulatory technical standards - e.g., if you're a large payment institution processing over a certain volume, or a bank designated as systemically important, etc., then you must do TLPT). In plain language: for instance, global systemically important banks, or trading venues with significant market share, etc., are in scope for TLPT.

Smaller organizations might not be forced to do TLPT, but they can still consider doing fewer intensive forms of red teaming voluntarily.

Now, how to conduct a TLPT successfully? The playbook breaks it into phases:

- Preparation Phase: This involves scoping the test with regulators. Uniquely, TLPT often requires regulatory approval of your test plan. You'll coordinate with your regulator to determine the scope (which critical functions will be tested), the rules of engagement (what's off-limits, like perhaps not touching certain extremely sensitive systems or customer data), and the external team to be used (typically an external certified red-team provider; DORA will likely require these testers to meet certain qualifications). You'll also gather *threat intelligence* - possibly hiring a threat intel provider - to craft realistic attack scenarios.
  For example, intelligence might say: "financial institutions like you are currently being targeted via VPN vulnerabilities and phishing for admin credentials." The scenario could then be simulating an attacker who first tries to breach via a phishing email, and if inside, attempts to move laterally and exfiltrate data or disrupt services. All this planning is documented in a test plan and often reviewed by the regulator before execution.
- Testing Phase: The red team goes to work according to the agreed plan. This could span several weeks. They will try multiple avenues to compromise your systems, just like real attackers, often working quietly to avoid detection.
  Meanwhile, your blue team is monitoring as usual. You want to see if and when they detect the intrusion. It's possible they might catch some steps (e.g., an alert on malware), or maybe not at all until the red team reaches their goal ("flags" like gaining domain admin or simulating a funds transfer).

- Closure (Reporting & Remediation) Phase: After the active test, there's a *replay* or debrief. Now the red team reveals what they did step by step, and the blue team (your defenders) discuss what they saw or missed. This is where the learning happens - maybe your monitoring missed a key indicator, or an internal process slowed down the response. A purple team exercise (collaboration between red and blue) is often done as part of closure, meaning the red and blue work together to replay some attack steps and ensure defenses are adjusted to catch them next time (hence "purple" - mixing red and blue). DORA's TLPT standards specifically encourage this collaborative learning in the aftermath. Finally, a detailed report is compiled. For regulatory compliance, you must document the scope, methods, findings (vulnerabilities found, controls bypassed), and remediation plans. Regulators might require this report or at least a summary to be submitted to them.

To prepare internally for TLPT so it doesn't wreak havoc talk about making sure you have backups and fail-safes in case the test inadvertently causes a system issue (for instance, if the red team is doing a denial-of-service simulation, you control the impact). We also advise on engaging the right external partners - firms that specialize in TLPT (some countries require using accredited providers). There's also the aspect of scope creep - ensuring the test is challenging but not so broad that it becomes unmanageable or dangerous.

We also discuss cost and logistics: TLPTs can be expensive and time-consuming, so planning in your budget and project timeline is key. But they are worth the insight gained. For example, a TLPT might reveal that while you had strong perimeter firewalls, once an attacker got in through a phishing email, your internal network had weak segmentation allowing them to traverse freely. That insight lets you invest in the right improvements (like better internal access controls) to prevent a real attacker from doing the same.

By providing a playbook for TLPT, we aim to demystify it. Yes, it's one of the most advanced things DORA asks for, but it's essentially a controlled fire drill. Just as building managers conduct fire drills to ensure everyone knows how to evacuate safely, TLPT is a cyber "fire drill" to ensure your security team and systems can handle a real attack. The chapter will include a sample mini-scenario and some do's and don'ts learned from TLPT exercises in the industry.

In conclusion, TLPT is about achieving assurance through simulation. It's a way to answer the tough question: "Can a determined hacker break into our systems?" by attempting it (with permission) and then reinforcing to avoid all the weaknesses found. Financial institutions that embrace TLPT tend to significantly boost their resilience - it's challenging, but the payoff is a much stronger defense and a team that's battle-tested.

Chapter 9: Pillar 4 - Managing Third-Party Risk

No bank or financial firm is an island; virtually all rely on third-party technology providers for critical operations. Pillar 4 of DORA zeroes in on ICT third-party risk management - making sure that outsourcing your tech doesn't mean outsourcing your risk and loosing oversight or control.

In this chapter, we explain DORA's comprehensive requirements for how to handle vendors, suppliers, and partners that provide you with IT services (from cloud data centers to software to payment processing platforms).

First, DORA requires financial entities to maintain a detailed inventory of all third-party ICT providers they use, especially mapping which business functions depend on which providers. This sounds basic, but many organizations are surprised to discover how many vendors they have contracts with and how interconnected those services are and often, how little knowledge and control they have over these.

A good inventory lists each provider, the services they supply, the data flows and handling and whether those services support any critical or important function of the firm and important contacts in case of an emergency. For example: *Provider X supplies cloud hosting for online banking (critical), Provider Y supplies email filtering (important but maybe not critical).* DORA also introduces the concept of identifying "critical ICT third-party service providers" from the financial entity's perspective. These are the providers that, if they fail, could severely impact your operations. There are criteria for this criticality assessment in Article 31 of DORA, including things like: how vital is the provider's service to your operations, how easily can you replace them (substitutability), and what impact would their failure have on you and potentially the wider financial system.

Once you know your critical providers, DORA mandates robust due diligence and risk assessment of those providers. This means before signing and regularly during the relationship, you should evaluate the provider's own risk posture: Do they have good security controls? Do they have business continuity plans? Will they notify you promptly of incidents? A lot of this might involve sending them questionnaires, requesting audit reports or certifications (like ISO 27001, SOC 2 reports), or even conducting onsite visits. If a cloud provider hosts your core banking, you better be sure they have top-notch physical and cyber security - regulators certainly expect you to verify it. However, some certifications only go as far as the certified entity wants to go and have documented in their quality manuals. These may not provide you with adequate risk management. A good example would be a provider that is ISO 27001 but does not require a copy of ID or a clean criminal record proof before letting their engineers work on your data or your systems.

The chapter will outline how to establish a Third-Party Risk Management (TPRM) framework in line with DORA. Key elements include:

- Risk tiering of suppliers: not all vendors are equal. You might categorize vendors as critical, important, or ordinary. The depth of risk management should be proportional (critical ones get very stringent oversight, minor ones less so).
- Contractual requirements: DORA is very specific about what must be in your contracts with ICT providers. Fr example, some m*andatory clauses* DORA expects: clear descriptions of services, uptime/service level agreements, data location and processing info, provisions for access and audit rights (so you or regulators can investigate if needed), incident assistance

(the vendor must assist you during an incident), participation in your resilience exercises, requirements to cooperate with authorities, and termination/exit rights. The exit strategy is crucial - you need the right to transition to another provider or bring services in-house without undue disruption if needed. We'll give examples of why these matters (imagine your provider suddenly has a major outage or regulatory ban; you may need to switch quickly).

- Ongoing monitoring: It's not set-and-forget after signing a contract. DORA expects continuous monitoring of the provider's performance and risk. This can include quarterly service reviews, tracking their compliance with service levels, annually updating their risk assessments, and staying alert to any news (like if the provider suffered a cyber incident elsewhere, or is getting acquired - anything that might change risk). You should maintain a register of all your outsourcing arrangements and report new ones to regulators yearly (DORA even requires an annual report to regulators about the number of new outsourcing arrangements, etc., for transparency).
- Concentration risk management: What if many firms rely on the same provider? DORA worries about systemic concentration (e.g., if all banks use one cloud provider and that provider fails, the entire sector is in trouble). So, regulators and firms will look at concentration risk. As an institution, you might consider not putting all critical services on one provider or at least having contingency plans if that provider goes down. Strategies like multi-cloud or backup providers vs. the complexity that introduces are important.

A significant novelty is that at the EU level, some providers will be officially designated as *Critical ICT Third-Party Providers* (CTPPs) for the whole financial sector. If, say, "MegaCloud Inc." is designated, then a European overseer (one of the ESAs) will directly supervise MegaCloud's resilience. In this chapter, we clarify that if you are a customer of a designated CTPP, you will have to ensure you cooperate with any oversight measures. For example, if the overseer asks MegaCloud for certain information about your contracts or usage, you might be involved. The idea is that regulators add an extra layer of scrutiny on big tech providers, but you still retain responsibility for your own risk management.

We also cover Fourth-party risk (your provider's subcontractors). DORA requires that you know if your provider is further outsourcing parts of the service (sub-outsourcing), and that critical subcontracting should be agreed by you. For instance, if your SaaS provider hosts data on a third-party cloud, you should know that and ideally have a say or at least be informed if they change that cloud provider.

A checklist for a DORA-compliant vendor management policy might include perform risk assessment before onboarding, include DORA clauses in contract, ensure data portability and exit strategy, require incident notification from vendor within X hours, annual security audit, etc. and for example, a scenario of how a failure in third-party risk can hurt (maybe referencing a real incident like the *Cloud provider outage that affected multiple banks*, to illustrate why these rules matter).

By mastering Pillar 4, an organization builds resilience not just within its own walls, but across its entire supply chain. The key takeaway is you can outsource services, but you cannot outsource responsibility. Under DORA, regulators will hold you accountable for failures at your vendor, so you must actively manage and mitigate that risk. Fortunately, following these requirements will significantly reduce the chance that a vendor issue catches you off guard.

Chapter 10: Pillar 5 - Information Sharing and Communication

The fifth pillar of DORA is often overlooked but is very important: Information Sharing. This pillar recognizes that no bank or firm can combat cyber threats alone. By sharing information about threats and vulnerabilities, the whole financial sector can become more resilient. In this chapter, we explain DORA's push for cooperation and intelligence-sharing within the financial ecosystem, and how organizations can participate.

DORA encourages financial entities to set up or join arrangements for sharing cyber threat information and best practices. What kind of information are we talking about? This could include warnings about new malware targeting banking apps, techniques hackers are using (Tactics, Techniques, and Procedures - TTPs), indicators of compromise (like malicious IP addresses, phishing email subjects, malware hashes), or lessons learned from incidents (e.g., "We experienced a ransomware attack, here's how the attackers got in and how we fixed it").

Why share? Because if one institution is hit or discovers a threat, sharing that intel can help others preempt or prepare for the same threat. Regulators see this as a way to prevent contagion: an attack on one doesn't easily spread to many if info is quickly shared.

DORA doesn't force you to share proprietary data or secrets - it emphasizes voluntary sharing under proper safeguards (especially confidentiality, so that sharing doesn't spook customers or reveal too much to adversaries). In fact, DORA calls for the creation of Information Sharing Arrangements (ISAs). These are agreements or platforms where financial firms can exchange cyber threat information among themselves securely. Many countries already have things like ISACs (Information Sharing and Analysis Centers) for finance. For example, there's the Financial Services ISAC (FS-ISAC) globally, and in Europe various central banks host exchange forums. DORA essentially endorses these and wants more firms to actively use them.

This chapter will suggest ways to engage in information sharing:

- Join industry groups: If an FS-ISAC or similar exists in your region, become a member. These groups often share anonymized alerts and reports. We provide a brief overview of how such groups work (they often have secure portals, regular meetings or calls, and a principle that information shared is not attributed to the sharer publicly).
- Share with authorities: Sometimes, regulators or CERTs (Computer Emergency Response Teams) act as hubs. For instance, a national CERT might gather incident reports from firms and circulate warnings. Responding to those or providing input when you can be part of being a good ecosystem citizen.
- Bilateral sharing: If you're a big bank, you might have peers you trust. DORA's spirit would support, say, two banks' CISOs picking up the phone if one sees something odd that might affect the other. Competition concerns often made banks siloed about incidents, but now the mindset is shifting to "we're all safer if we collaborate on cyber defense."

Internal communication as part of this pillar. DORA requires that within an organization, there are clear lines of communication for cyber matters. For example, how does an operational incident get communicated from the IT ops team to business leadership? Do you have an internal alert system (like SMS or email blast) to quickly inform staff or key teams of major disruptions? DORA wants firms to not fall apart in silos during a crisis. So, an incident affecting, say, online brokerage should be promptly communicated to customer support teams (so they can handle calls) and to PR teams (to manage public info) in addition to the IT team fixing it.

Building a culture of information sharing is also stressed. This means encouraging your teams to report near-misses or small cyber issues internally without fear. If an employee nearly fell for a phishing email, do they feel safe to tell IT, "Hey I clicked something suspicious," so that the team can investigate? That internal sharing mentality helps catch incidents early.

The chapter provides examples of success through sharing: perhaps recount a scenario like "Bank A shares intel about a phishing campaign targeting credit card data; Bank B, upon hearing this, finds and blocks similar emails - avoiding a breach." On the flip side, not sharing can have costs: if everyone stays mum about attacks, attackers can reuse the same methods on multiple institutions.

We also mention that sharing is not one-way - it's about receiving intel too. By participating, you'll get access to a wealth of information. To manage it, many firms use threat intelligence feeds or platforms. We won't get too technical but might note that specialized tools can automatically integrate shared indicators into your security systems (for instance, auto-blocking an IP that an ISAC alert flagged as malicious).

Lastly, we address confidentiality and legal aspects: DORA clarifies that sharing under these arrangements should respect data protection and confidentiality laws.

You wouldn't share customer data, for example, just the threat specifics. Often info is anonymized ("Bank X" becomes "a European bank"). Also, there might be concerns about reputational risk in admitting incidents - but if done within a trusted circle, the benefits outweigh those fears. Regulators themselves may facilitate anonymous sharing.

In conclusion, Pillar 5 is about collective defense. While Pillars 1-4 focus on what *your institution* does internally, Pillar 5 looks outward and says, “Let’s team up.” A cybercriminal attacking one bank is likely probing others too; through sharing, the community can mount a unified defense. We encourage readers to treat information sharing not as an afterthought but as an essential piece of their resilience strategy. One firm’s detection can become every firm’s prevention if communicated swiftly. That kind of sector-wide resilience is exactly what DORA hopes to achieve.

Part 3: The Consultant's Roadmap

Part 3 shifts perspective: now that we've explained the "what" of DORA, we get practical about the "how." Written from a project manager or a consultant's point of view, these chapters walk you through implementing DORA in an organization. We cover the journey from initial assessment, through creating a remediation plan, to embedding resilience in everyday operations. We also prepare you for audits and highlight the importance of communication in gaining buy-in. Consider this the project plan for achieving DORA compliance.

Chapter 11: DORA Gap Analysis - Assessing Your Readiness

What is a gap analysis? It's a systematic review of each DORA requirement, checking whether you meet it, partially meet it, or not at all, and documenting the gaps. The output is a clear list of what needs improvement. We'll guide you on how to do this effectively.

Step 1: Gather DORA's key requirements. Conveniently, we've outlined them in Parts 1 and 2 of this book. In practice, one might use a checklist drawn from the regulation or RTS (Regulatory Technical Standards). For example, list items like "Do we have a documented ICT risk management framework? Y/N", "Do we conduct annual testing and have we done TLPT if required? Y/N", "Do contracts with critical suppliers include XYZ clauses? Y/N", and so on.

Step 2: Conduct a Security and Resilience Review. This means engaging the relevant teams in your organization to collect evidence. You'll likely interview IT managers, security officers, business continuity planners, etc., and review documentation they have. Key areas to review include:

- Policies and procedures (do you have ones covering ICT risk, incident response, third-party risk, etc. and are they up to date?).
- Technological measures (do you use proper access management, encryption, monitoring tools?).
- Incident and crisis management setup (do you have an incident response plan and has it been tested?).
- Inventory of assets and third parties (is it complete and maintained?).
- Past incidents or audit findings (did they reveal weaknesses not yet fixed?).
- Roles and responsibilities (is it clear who handles what in

ICT risk?).

We provide a sample gap analysis template in this chapter, possibly as a table:

Requirement | Current Status | Gap? | Notes/Action needed.

For instance: "Board oversight of ICT risk - Board receives quarterly IT risk report? - Current: Board only gets annual report - Gap: frequency and content need enhancement - Action: increase reporting to quarterly with metrics X, Y."

Focus areas: We suggest focusing on key security aspects during the gap review:

- Access management: Are there strong controls on who can access critical systems (MFA, least privilege, etc.)?
- Information security roles: Do you have defined security officer, etc., and is their mandate clear?
- Vulnerability management: Is there a process to regularly patch and address vulnerabilities?
- Third-party risk: Do we have a list of providers and a process to assess them?
- Incident handling: have incidents happened and were they handled ad hoc or via established process?

Often, a maturity model approach is useful: maybe rank each area 1-5. For example, "Incident Response: Level 2 (informal process, some documentation but not fully tested). Need to reach Level 4 (formal process, regular drills, meets DORA standards)."

Leveraging automation: The chapter also hints that doing a gap analysis manually can be laborious. Some companies use automated tools or software to scan compliance posture. For instance, a tool might scan configurations or check policy documents to identify missing elements. While not required, such tools can speed up work, especially in large IT environments (one might use them to find all instances of outdated software, etc. as part of risk identification). But even with tools, human judgment is key.

When performing the gap analysis, engage stakeholders from all relevant departments. The IT security team, IT operations, risk management, compliance, business continuity, procurement (for vendor contracts) - all will have pieces of the puzzle. The process of gathering info for the gap analysis is itself an awareness exercise. You might do workshops or questionnaires with them. We provide tips on interviewing: e.g., how to ask an open question like "How do we track ICT incidents currently?" to see if there's a formal log and process or if it's ad hoc.

After data gathering, analyze and document gaps: maybe you find, for example, that you have decent cyber security tools (firewalls, etc.) but lack an overarching ICT risk policy and board reporting - that's a gap under Pillar 1 governance. Or you might find you have incident management down pat but never considered TLPT - that's a gap under Pillar 3 advanced testing. Document each gap with clear description and the impact. The regulator's perspective is useful: which gaps would they consider most critical? Usually anything related to major incident handling or lacking board oversight would be high priority.

Finally, we stress the need to prioritize gaps. A gap analysis often uncovers dozens of items. Not all are equal. Use risk-based thinking to prioritize. Perhaps rank gaps as High (must fix before DORA takes effect or soon after because they're critical), Medium, Low. High might include things like "No incident reporting procedure to regulator exists" - that's critical. Low might be "some minor policy wording not aligned" which can wait.

The chapter may include a short fictional example: e.g., *FinBank's DORA readiness check found 15 gaps. High priorities included lack of a formal third-party register and no cyber incident communication plan. Low priority gaps included not yet joining an information-sharing network.* This helps illustrate outcome.

By the end of this chapter, the reader should know how to execute a thorough DORA readiness assessment. Furthermore, implementation Planning, because once you know the gaps, you can plan projects to close them. We make the point that investing time in a good gap analysis will save time and resources later, by focusing efforts where needed and providing a baseline to measure progress (you can later show how gaps closed over time). Essentially: *measure twice, cut once.* Assess first, then fix.

Chapter 12: The DORA Implementation Plan

Armed with the results of the gap analysis, we now focus on building a DORA Implementation Plan. This chapter is about translating those identified gaps into a concrete, phased action plan to achieve compliance. Think of it as the project roadmap for the next 6, 12, or 18 months (or however long until your organization is DORA-ready).

Prioritize and Scope the work: We start by prioritizing the gaps identified. Typically, you'd tackle high-risk/high-impact gaps first. For example, if the gap analysis revealed that incident response procedures are lacking, that's something to fix early on, since a major incident could happen any time. On the other hand, if you need to enhance some documentation details, that might be later. We talk about considering any regulatory deadlines - DORA came into application on 17 Jan 2025, but some technical standards or specific requirements might have staggered dates or grace periods. Plan around those; if something must be done by a certain date legally, that's priority.

Define workstreams or projects: It helps to group related gaps into workstreams. For instance:

- Workstream 1: Governance & Strategy - address board oversight, policy creation/update, roles and responsibilities.
- Workstream 2: Technology & Security Enhancements - implement or upgrade tools for monitoring, access control, etc.
- Workstream 3: Incident & Continuity Planning - establish incident management plan, run BC/DR drills.
- Workstream 4: Third-Party Risk Management - build the vendor register, update contracts, set oversight process.
- Workstream 5: Testing & TLPT - develop testing program

and plan a TLPT if needed.

- Workstream 6: Training & Awareness - ensure staff know new procedures, run awareness sessions (e.g., phishing tests as part of resilience).

  Each workstream will have specific tasks.

Phased approach: The plan should be broken into phases with milestones. For example:

- Phase 1 (next 3 months): Quick wins and foundational tasks - e.g., assign DORA compliance owner, form project team, start drafting missing policies, kick off vendor inventory.
- Phase 2 (3-6 months): Medium-term fixes - e.g., complete risk assessment updates, implement new monitoring tool, conduct training, initiate any needed procurement (like if you need a new backup solution by installing modern Synthetic Back up systems for example).
- Phase 3 (6-12 months): Complex tasks - e.g., execute TLPT, fully test BCP/DR, finalize contract addendums with third parties.
- Phase 4 (by DORA effective date or internal deadline): Final gap closures, documentation collation, management sign-offs, and maybe a mock audit to ensure readiness.

Resource allocation and budgeting including how to estimate the effort and cost for each part. For instance, if you need to perform a TLPT, you'll budget for external specialists. If you need a new software (like a GRC tool or incident reporting system), account for that. Also, internal manpower: maybe you need a full-time project manager or you'll borrow people from IT, risk, etc. We suggest drawing up a responsibility matrix (RACI) for tasks - who's Responsible, Accountable, Consulted, Informed or better still a PRACI, whereas the 'P' is the person or team who performs the actual IT or other function. Updating policies might be led by Compliance (Responsible), with IT Security consulted, and board informed.

You will need also to cover project governance: how to keep the implementation on track. Regular progress meetings, status reports to senior management, risk logs (the project itself can have risks, like delay in tool implementation or resistance to change in culture).

Strong governance might a CRAB, a Change request Advisory Board, a RAB, Risk Advisory Board and also entail a steering committee (including some execs or board members for oversight - since DORA is board's duty, having a board sponsor is wise).

Setting measurable targets: We recommend making the action plan measurable. For example, "By Q2, incident response plan updated and 2 drills conducted" or "By June, 100% of critical vendor contracts reviewed for DORA clauses." These give clear checkpoints. DORA compliance is not just binary but having these KPIs will show progress and help ensure nothing slips through cracks.

Budgeting: DORA compliance has costs but also consider the cost of not doing things (fines, incidents). Being DORA compliant is also like an insurance policy whre you incur costs hoping never to have to declare an incident or accident. Make sure youcan justify budget to management: highlight that some expenses (like better monitoring tools or backup systems) not only meet DORA but also reduce risk of loss. In other words, it's an investment in resilience that likely saves money by preventing incidents or downtime. Also mention penalties: up to 2% of turnover fine vs. investing maybe 0.1% in improvements - better to invest now than pay later.

Integrate with existing projects: Maybe your company already has ongoing IT risk improvements or is working on NIS2 or GDPR projects. We suggest finding synergies. For example, if there's a digital transformation project upgrading systems, incorporate resilience requirements in it. Or if you recently did a GDPR project creating incident notification processes, use that knowledge for DORA's incident requirements. This avoids reinventing the wheel and can save time/money.

Include a hypothetical timeline or Gantt chart outline (if not visually, described in text): Month 1-2 do X, Month 3-4 do Y, etc., culminating in a compliance date.

Change management: Implementation isn't just technical; it involves people and processes. Discuss the need to manage change: communicate changes early to those affected, provide training (e.g., if you introduce a new incident reporting form or tool, train staff on it), update job descriptions if needed (maybe the CIO now explicitly must report to board quarterly on ICT risks - that should be formalized). Encourage a culture where these new practices are accepted, not seen as burdensome compliance red-tape.

By laying out an implementation plan clearly, it also helps to avoid overwhelm. Seeing the journey in structured phases can reassure management and technical staff that it's feasible. Yes, DORA is extensive, systemic and can be daunting at first but with a plan you can tackle it piece by piece.

A short example of a plan can look something like this: *ACME Bank's DORA Project Plan included Phase 1: Create policies and governance by March; Phase 2: Tech upgrades Apr-Jun; Phase 3: Testing and drill Jul-Sep; Phase 4: Final adjustments Oct-Dec. They appointed a project lead and reported progress to the Risk Committee monthly. As a result, they hit all milestones and were ready by the deadline.* This narrative illustrates how planning pays off.

In summary, turn theory into action. Ensures that after reading about what needs to be done, you know how to list, organize and execute those tasks systematically.

With a solid implementation plan, you set the stage for sustainable compliance rather than last-minute scrambling.

Chapter 13: The Continuous Resilience Cycle

Achieving DORA compliance isn't a one-time project; it's about baking resilience into the day-to-day operations of the organization. We discuss how to embed DORA requirements into business-as-usual processes and establish a cycle of continuous improvement in digital operational resilience. This ensures that once you've implemented changes, you don't just put the binder on a shelf - you keep living it, adapting and improving over time.

We introduce the concept of a Continuous Resilience and Improvement Cycle, which can be likened to Lean Management and the Deming Cycle (Plan-Do-Check-Act) or similar continuous improvement models. Such techniques can become part of DevOps which is based on many Lean principles and release plans of any upgrades, changes etc.:

- Plan: Continuously maintain and update your ICT risk management plans and resilience strategies. For example, every year (or whenever there's a major change in the business or threat landscape), review your risk assessments and plans. Set objectives for improvements (e.g., "this year, reduce average incident response time by 20%" or "implement new backup solution for quicker recovery").
- Do: Carry out the resilience activities regularly. This means running your tests, doing your trainings, monitoring systems, etc. It also includes following the processes established: if an incident happens, you *use the DORA-designed process* to handle it (not an ad hoc scramble). Day-to-day tasks like reviewing logs, updating patches, conducting vendor reviews all contribute to resilience.

- Check: Monitor and audit how well you're doing. This could be internal audits of DORA controls, periodic reporting of resilience metrics to management, and lessons learned exercises. For instance, schedule quarterly or semi-annual reviews: "How many incidents did we have? Did we report them properly? What went well, what didn't?" If you conduct a TLPT or a drill, do a post-mortem and document findings. Also, check compliance: ensure your documentation is up to date, and if any new regulatory guidelines are issued (since DORA will evolve with technical standards, etc.), incorporate them.
- Act (Adapt): Based on what you observe in the "Check" step, make improvements. If an audit finds a deficiency, fix it. If a test reveals a new vulnerability, patch it and perhaps update the test plan. If the threat landscape changes (say, a wave of supply chain attacks hits the industry), adapt your controls and maybe do a special scenario test for that.

By going through Plan-Do-Check-Act continuously, you maintain a resilience program rather than a one-off compliance task.

We emphasize that regulatory compliance is not static. Regulations like DORA might get updated technical standards; regulators may issue new guidance or expectations. Moreover, your business might change - maybe you launch a new digital service or adopt a new cloud technology, which introduces new risks. The continuous cycle means you factor those in. For example, if you start using a new critical third-party provider, your third-party risk process should automatically kick in (do due diligence, add to register, monitor them) rather than waiting for an annual review.

A key piece of continuous resilience is building it into governance structures. We suggest organizations have an ongoing Operational Resilience or ICT Risk Committee that meets regularly (say monthly or quarterly) to review all things resilience: incident reports, status of improvement actions, upcoming tests, changes in ICT inventory, etc. This keeps leadership engaged beyond the initial compliance push.

Another aspect: culture and awareness. Continuity means employees-from the IT team to business units-remain aware of their roles in resilience. This might involve periodic training refreshers (cybersecurity awareness training yearly, incident drill for crisis team every year, etc.). Encourage a culture of *reporting issues*: if staff continually report near-misses or suggest improvements, that feeds the cycle.

Keeping documentation up to date is part of continuity. For example, if you change a process, update the policy document now, not "later" (which often never comes). That way, when audit time comes, you're not panicking to overhaul stale docs.

Metrics and KPIs are important to sustaining momentum. We suggest establishing key indicators for resilience and tracking them over time. Some examples:

- Number of major incidents per quarter (and aim to reduce or keep low).
- Average time to detect incidents (MTTD) and respond/ recover (MTTR).
- Percentage of critical systems tested as planned (e.g., 100% of critical systems had at least one DR test this year).
- Vendor risk assessments completed (%).
- Training completion rates for relevant staff.

These can be reported in a dashboard to executives. Seeing metrics helps drive continuous improvements ("We're still too slow in detecting incidents; let's invest in better monitoring" or "Our vendor reviews are lagging, need to assign more resources").

We mention integrating DORA cycle with other frameworks: Many financial firms may integrate DORA's cycle with their Enterprise

Risk Management or Operational Risk cycles. For instance, include ICT risk in the overall risk register, ensure it's part of enterprise risk reporting, etc. It should not be siloed.

By establishing a continuous cycle, the organization essentially future-proofs itself. DORA compliance then becomes *sustainable.* Also, when regulators come, they'll want to see evidence of this continuous improvement ethos. If you can show, for example, that every year you improved on some metrics or closed prior findings, it gives confidence that you're on top of things.

We could include an anecdote: *One year after initial DORA compliance, XYZ Bank didn't stop there. They held quarterly cyber drills, and the board continued to get regular updates. When a new malware threat emerged targeting banks, XYZ quickly incorporated indicators from peers (Pillar 5) and updated their controls. As a result, they avoided an incident that hit some less-prepared competitors.* This illustrates how continuous focus yields dividends.

In summary, don't treat DORA like a tick-the-box project that ends on a deadline. Instead, treat it as the new normal for how you operate. Integrate recurring activities and adapt your DORA related GRC (Governance Risk and Compliance) to all related changs and projects. By doing so, not only do you remain compliant, but you genuinely strengthen your operational resilience, which is the whole point of DORA in the first place. The continuous resilience cycle turns initial compliance efforts into lasting business-as-usual practices that keep your organization safe and sound.

Chapter 14: Audits and Documentation

This chapter highlights the importance of being audit-ready and maintaining thorough documentation for all your digital operational resilience measures. Under DORA, you should expect that at some point, either internal or external auditors - and certainly regulators - will want to verify that you are doing what you say you're doing. Good documentation and audit preparation are like your insurance policy to prove compliance and spot issues proactively.

Documentation is your friend (not just paperwork for its own sake). DORA requires clear and comprehensive documentation for many areas:

- You need policies (for ICT risk management, incident management, etc.).
- You need inventories (of assets, third-party providers, etc.).
- Incident logs and reports must be kept.
- Testing plans, scenarios, and results should be documented.
- Training records, meeting minutes (e.g., of risk committees), and audit logs.

  Essentially, if it's not written down, regulators may not consider it done.

A DORA Documentation Checklist can look like this:

- ICT Risk Management Framework document - describing governance, processes, risk appetite, etc.
- Business Impact Analysis (BIA) and Risk Assessment reports - showing you identified critical functions and related risks.
- Incident response plan and record of incidents - including those reports to regulators we mentioned.
- Testing schedule and reports - including TLPT report,

vulnerability scan results, etc., along with remediation follow-up.

- Third-party register and copies of critical contracts or at least key clauses evidence.
- Information sharing logs - e.g., if you participate in ISAC, note significant alerts you received or shared.
- Training materials and attendance - evidence that staff were trained on these new policies.
- Audit reports - any internal audits done on ICT resilience and how you addressed findings.

Some create a shared and secured access folder system or documentation system where each of the above area is separately included and all relative documentation can be found there. You can adapt it to your way of working and your needs.

Now, about Audits: We differentiate a bit between internal audits and external/regulatory audits:

- Internal Audit (or an internal self-assessment): Ideally, before a regulator ever audits you, your internal audit function (if you have one) or an equivalent independent reviewer should assess DORA compliance. They will check the documentation, interview people, maybe sample a few controls (like see if an incident drill was done, or spot-check if a vendor's file has all necessary docs).
- We suggest collaborating with internal audit early - give them the DORA requirements and let them evaluate readiness. This helps catch any oversight. It's better the internal team finds a gap and you fix it, than the regulator finding it later.
- External Audits/Regulatory Inspections: Regulators might conduct a focused ICT risk exam. They may send a questionnaire first (asking for many of the documents above),

then come on-site (or virtual) for interviews, and they might even do their own testing (some regulators have been known to ask for a simulated incident or walk-through). We described earlier the supervisory approach, and here we prepare the reader for the practicalities of an audit day.

We provide a checklist to prepare for a DORA audit:

1. Make sure all your documentation is up to date and readily accessible. If you scramble to find documents when an auditor asks, it gives a bad impression. Better to have a structured repository binder labeled "DORA Compliance Documentation".
2. Do a mock audit: Rehearse answering likely questions. For example, an auditor might ask, "Show us evidence of board involvement in ICT risk oversight" - you could show meeting minutes where the board discussed and approved the ICT risk strategy or "How do you classify incidents as major?" - you produce the criteria and an example of a recent incident classification and report.
3. Ensure key personnel are available and briefed. The auditor will likely want to talk to the CISO, the CIO, maybe the COO or risk officer, and some operational staff. Those people should know what DORA is (hopefully through this project they do) and be consistent in their answers. We advise holding an internal prep meeting so everyone understands what's been implemented and where things are documented.
4. Be honest and transparent. If something is still work in progress, it's better to say "We have a plan and it's 80% done, here's the timeline" than to pretend all is perfect. Regulators appreciate candor and evidence of progress. However, try not to have glaring gaps by audit time. That's what the earlier chapters help avoid.

We stress the importance of maintaining audit trails and logs of DORA related activities. In the case of digital logs and software generated logs make sure these are backed up and are available. In case of incidents including ransomware these digital and other logs if not backed up may be lost and are a very valuable tool to track what happened and how it happened. Hackers always try to erase such logs and a good back up system can be a life saver.

For instance, when you do an incident drill, keep the attendee list, agenda, and outcome report. When you update a policy, keep version history. If an incident happened, preserve the records of what you did and communications. If you had exceptions (like a test that couldn't be done as planned), note why and the mitigation. These details can save you if ever questioned later ("Why wasn't there a TLPT this cycle?" - "Because we had X merger, but here's approval from regulator to postpone until next quarter" – documented and saved!).

Common pitfalls to avoid: We discuss a few:

- Documentation exists but is not used in practice (audit will catch if employees are unaware of a fancy policy document). Avoid creating shelfware - ensure processes match what's written.
- Overcomplicating documentation - e.g., 100-page policies that nobody reads. Keep them clear and user-friendly and better have checklists with results when used and mitigations documented.
- Forgetting to update after changes. For example, you change a cloud provider but your register wasn't updated - that's a gap.
- Not retaining evidence of compliance activities. If you fix a vulnerability, keep the ticket or scan report showing it's fixed. Add a record to your DORA activities log.

A good practice is periodic self-checks: maybe every year do an internal review of DORA controls to see if they still meet requirements and produce a report to management.

A sample audit Q&A scenario to make it tangible:

Auditor asks: "How do you ensure your critical third-party providers are resilient?"

Your possible answer (supported with docs): "We maintain a third-party risk framework. Here is our register of providers, highlighting critical ones. For each, we require annual compliance attestations and we've included all DORA-required clauses in contracts (see sample contract excerpt). We also performed a continuity test with Provider X last year - here's the report."

Auditor: "What happens if that provider fails?"

You: "We have an exit strategy and backup provider ready for our core services. It's documented in our outsourcing policy and we rehearse transition in scenario tests. Here's the summary of our last exercise where we simulated Provider X outage."

Such thorough responses with evidence will likely satisfy them.

Finally, we underscore that good documentation and audit preparedness is not just about pleasing regulators; it also helps the organization itself. It brings clarity, preserves institutional knowledge (important when staff leave, etc.), and helps you track progress. In crisis situations, having clear docs (like an incident playbook) can be literally life-saving for the business. So, invest in documentation as a core part of resilience.

In summary, a checklist and mindset: *document everything, audit yourself before others do, and be ready to demonstrate your resilience measures at any time.* DORA compliance is as much about evidencing what you do as it is about doing it.

Chapter 15: The Strategic Communication Plan

Here we deal with something often overlooked in technical projects: communication. Having a great resilience program won't succeed if people aren't on board or if stakeholders are left in the dark. This chapter provides guidance on how to communicate DORA initiatives and ongoing resilience efforts to various audiences - employees, management/board, and external partners - to ensure buy-in and cooperation.

Internal communication (employees at all levels):

Everyone in the organization plays a role in operational resilience, whether they know it or not. The plan needs to be communicated in a way that staff understand how DORA affects them. For instance:

- Conduct an internal awareness campaign about DORA: maybe a townhall meeting or an intranet blog by the CEO or CIO explaining that "We're implementing DORA - here's why it matters (to keep our services reliable and secure) and what changes to expect." Emphasize it's not just a regulatory burden, but a beneficial strengthening of the company.
- Tailor communications to different groups. Tech teams need detailed info about new procedures; general staff might just need high-level awareness (like "if you see something cyber-odd, report it; we're bolstering systems behind the scenes").
- Use engaging formats: Some companies gamify cybersecurity training (phishing simulations with feedback, etc.). Or use infographics to show new incident reporting flow, etc.
- Explain new policies in simple terms. If you roll out an updated incident escalation chart, publish it on the intranet and maybe do a short info session on how to use it.
- Solicit feedback: employees might have insights on where

operations are fragile or suggestions to improve processes. A culture that encourages speaking up will only enhance resilience.

Board and executive communication:

While earlier we stressed the board's duties, here we talk about how to keep the board and top management engaged and supportive. Tips include:

- Regular updates: Provide concise, meaningful reports to the board (maybe at each quarterly meeting) on DORA project progress and thereafter on resilience status. Use metrics and highlight improvements as well as any concerns.
  You can use also a one pager PowerPoint slide with:
  - Accomplished Activities
  - Planned Activities
  - Current Activities
  - Recommendations
  - Roadblocks & Risks
- Frame communication in business terms: For CEOs and business leaders, explain how resilience ties to business performance and reputation ("Our uptime is part of customer trust. DORA helps us ensure uptime, which keeps customers and revenue.").
- Share success stories: Once you have wins (like "our new incident response plan helped resolve a recent outage in 30% less time"), let leadership know. It reinforces the value of the program.
- Be honest about resource needs: If you require budget or staff to implement something, present a case early with clear justification.

External partners communication:

This includes communication with third-party providers and potentially with customers or the public when appropriate.

- For third-party vendors: It's important to communicate your expectations early. For example, reach out to critical ICT providers and let them know, "Due to DORA, we'll need to update our contract to include X clauses" or "We will be asking for XYZ information annually." Some vendors might not be aware of DORA details; proactive communication avoids surprises and friction. Approach it as a partnership to improve resilience together.
- Also, engage in dialogue: ask key providers about their continuity plans or if they are prepping for oversight (if they suspect being designated critical). The more you build a collaborative relationship, the better they'll support you in crises.
- For clients/customers: Usually customers don't need to know the nitty-gritty of DORA, but they do care about service reliability and data safety. Communicate commitments like, "Bank ABC is investing heavily in digital resilience to ensure you can rely on our services anytime." Marketing can even turn DORA compliance into a trust point (e.g., mentioning adherence to strict EU resilience standards in brochures).
- Also, plan how you'd communicate externally during incidents as part of PR. Under DORA, if a big incident happens, you'll inform customers if they're affected. Having pre-drafted holding statements or a crisis comms plan is wise. E.g., "In the unlikely event of a cyber incident causing a service outage, we have communications ready to assure customers we're on it."

Cross-industry communication:

This tie back to Pillar 5, but from a comms standpoint: ensure you're plugged into industry forums and consider joint communications if appropriate. For example, via industry associations, communicate general readiness or share non-sensitive info on threats.

Change management needs good communication: People naturally resist change, especially if it adds tasks or seems to critique past practices. The strategic comm plan should frame DORA changes positively:

- "This is about improving, not finding fault."
- Highlight how these efforts protect everyone's job security in a sense (a big cyber incident could harm the company).
- Recognize and celebrate milestones: When the first TLPT is successfully completed, for example, thank the teams involved and share key outcomes (minus sensitive details) so everyone sees progress.

Tone and style:

We advise communications to be clear, jargon-free (or explain acronyms like ICT, TLPT in simple terms as needed), and consistent. Mixed messages can confuse-so coordinate messaging across departments. The plan could involve the corporate communications team or HR to ensure alignment.

One practical tip: create a "DORA Champions" network - identify people in different departments who are enthusiastic or knowledgeable about resilience and have them act as liaisons or ambassadors. They can help communicate to their teams in their language and gather feedback.

Finally, show that this is a continuous commitment, not a one-off. For example, incorporate DORA/resilience updates in the company newsletter periodically, not just during project rollout.

As an example, a mini-case: *A mid-size bank launched an internal campaign called "Operation Resilience" with a cool logo and regular emails highlighting different pillars, tips for staff, etc. They noticed increased incident reporting by employees and faster adoption of new security tools as a result. Conversely, a peer that just sent one policy email saw confusion and slower uptake.* This illustrates the payoff of good communication.

In summary, human factors are critical. You need people-from top to bottom and even outside your org-to understand, support, and participate in the DORA journey. A strategic communication plan ensures everyone is rowing in the same direction. Good communication can transform compliance from a chore into a shared mission to protect and empower the business.

Part 4: Beyond the Regulation

In Part 4, we step back from the compliance checklist and look at the bigger picture. We explore practical examples of DORA in action across different organizations, relate DORA to longstanding business continuity practices, discuss the ramifications of ignoring these requirements, and finally, paint a vision of the benefits gained by fully embracing digital operational resilience. This part reinforces that DORA isn't just about avoiding fines - it's about thriving in a risk-filled digital age.

Chapter 16: DORA in Action - Case Studies

This chapter brings theory to life by presenting case studies of how DORA can be applied in different types of financial entities. We illustrate, through realistic (albeit fictionalized) scenarios, what implementing DORA looks like for a large bank versus a small fintech startup, and possibly other contrasts (like an insurance company or asset manager) to show the flexibility and impact of the regulation.

Case Study 1: BigBank Inc. (Large Global Bank)

Profile: BigBank is a multinational bank with millions of customers, multiple lines of business (retail, corporate, investment banking), and a complex IT environment including legacy systems and cutting-edge digital platforms. It has thousands of employees and an extensive outsourcing landscape (cloud providers, core banking software vendors, etc.).

DORA Journey Highlights:

- **Scope & Governance:** BigBank immediately recognized it's squarely in DORA's scope and appointed a Board-level committee to oversee the DORA program. They even added a new board member with cyber expertise to help meet the "Board's new duty".
- **Risk Management Framework:** The bank had an existing operational risk framework, but DORA prompted an overhaul of the ICT risk section. They mapped critical business services (like ATM network, online banking, international payments) to underlying IT systems and teams. A comprehensive risk register was developed, showing, for example, that the online banking service depends on System A (in-house) and Cloud Service B (vendor). For each, threats

and controls were listed.

- **Incident Example:** During their DORA prep, BigBank suffered a significant incident - a data center power outage that took some services offline for 3 hours. The case study describes how their (improved) incident management process kicked in: the incident response team convened within minutes, fallback systems were activated, and internal communications kept everyone updated. Because of DORA awareness, they classified it properly as a major incident and notified regulators within the same day (rather than hiding it). They later filed a thorough report, which the regulators appreciated, and got feedback that their response was well-handled.
- **TLPT at BigBank:** BigBank, being large, underwent a TLPT. The scenario might be a simulated attack on their wholesale payments system. We describe how this test uncovered a weakness (e.g., the red team managed to breach an old legacy system that hadn't been well-monitored, pivoting into the payment network). BigBank took it as a wake-up call, promptly investing to segment that network and decommission the legacy vulnerability. The case shows TLPT value.
- **Third-Party Risk:** BigBank identified 5 "critical" ICT providers they rely on (a major cloud provider, a core banking software vendor, a payments network, etc.). They set up quarterly risk meetings with each and renegotiated contracts to include the DORA clauses like access and audit rights. In one instance, a provider was initially resistant to an audit clause, but BigBank leveraged their importance (and the regulation's backing) to insist - resulting in better transparency. During a later industry-wide cloud outage,

BigBank had contingency plans with another provider, minimizing downtime, whereas some competitors were caught off guard.

- **Information Sharing:** BigBank joined the FS-ISAC for threat intel. The case might mention how they received a heads-up about a new strain of banking malware targeting mobile apps and proactively fortified their systems and alerted customers on safe practices, potentially avoiding an incident.
- **Outcome:** BigBank's size meant high effort, but also high capability. By the time DORA went live, they had a robust resilience program that not only ticked the compliance boxes but demonstrably reduced their incident frequency and improved response. The case can conclude with BigBank's COO saying something like, "DORA made us examine ourselves rigorously. It wasn't easy, but now we're more confident in our operational stability than ever. It's become a competitive strength when dealing with regulators and clients."

Case Study 2: FinStart Ltd. (Small Fintech Payment Provider)

Profile: FinStart is a startup providing a mobile payment app, operating in a couple of EU countries. It has 50 employees, mainly developers, and heavily uses cloud services (no physical data center of its own). FinStart is innovative and agile but doesn't have the layers of departments a big bank has - often engineers double-hat as operations/ security.

DORA Journey Highlights:

- **Initial Reaction:** FinStart's CEO learns about DORA maybe through an industry newsletter and realizes they fall under "payment service providers" subject to it. Initially, there's concern: "We don't have a big risk team, how do we do all this?" They consider hiring a consultant for guidance (a scenario where a small firm might lean on external help).

- **Right-Sizing the Framework:** The case shows that even a small firm can apply DORA in a proportionate way. They assign one of their senior engineers to be the "DORA champion" to coordinate compliance. They draft a lean ICT risk policy - maybe 5 pages - that outlines key roles (even if one person fills many) and key procedures appropriate for their size. DORA allows proportional application (simplified framework for smaller entities as noted in Article 16), so FinStart uses that to not over-complicate things.
- **Risk Assessment:** FinStart has fewer systems and mostly one major product, so mapping critical functions is straightforward (the app backend and the payment processing connection). They identify biggest risks as cyberattacks and cloud outages. They implement some relatively simple but effective controls: e.g., require all employees to do 2FA, contract a managed security service to monitor their cloud environment since they don't have 24/7 staff.
- **Incident Approach:** Perhaps FinStart hasn't had a major incident yet (fingers crossed), but they set up an on-call rotation and a Slack channel for incident response so they can react fast. They pre-draft an incident report template. When a minor incident (like a short service glitch due to a software bug) happens, they treat it as a test, documenting how they fixed it and doing a post-mortem. This prepares them for bigger issues.
- **Third-Party dependency:** FinStart's biggest third-party is the cloud provider hosting their app. They might also use

third-party libraries and an email service. They don't have leverage to heavily negotiate with, say, a giant cloud provider, but they do carefully read the provider's terms and ensure they align with DORA expectations (for example, the cloud's SLA and security certifications). The case might show FinStart opting to multi-region deploy on the cloud to improve resilience because they can't demand much contract change. For smaller vendors (like a third-party library support contract), they incorporate some basic DORA terms.

- **Testing on a budget:** FinStart can't afford full TLPT in-house, but since they might not be mandated (only larger players are mandated for TLPT, FinStart likely falls below thresholds), they still do some testing: they use open-source tools for vulnerability scanning, engage an external firm for an annual penetration test on their app, and do a restore-from-backup drill to ensure they can rebuild their system if needed. The chapter highlights that you don't need millions to test - smart utilization of available tools goes a long way.
- **Information sharing and help:** FinStart joins a local fintech association where cybersecurity is discussed. Through that, they learn from peers and perhaps piggyback on sector initiatives (maybe the central bank offers a cyber range exercise for FinTech's, which they join). They also decide to subscribe to a threat intel newsletter - so at least they stay aware of current threats.
- **Outcome:** By the end, FinStart has turned what could have been an overwhelming mandate into a manageable set of practices. The CEO finds that having these in place actually helps when pitching to business clients or regulators: they can demonstrate reliability. If a regulator questions them,

they can show their small but robust policies, incident logs, etc. Perhaps we note that FinStart's size meant fewer boxes to tick but still required a cultural shift - the developers now think about security and continuity as part of their coding and deployment (BusDevSecOps mindset).

Additional cases (optional/brief):

We could briefly mention another type like an insurance company or Asset manager:

- Insurance Co: Focus might be on how they integrated DORA with Solvency II risk management, how they worry about policyholder data and outages of underwriting systems, etc.
- Asset Manager: Might highlight reliance on market data providers and trading systems, and how DORA is implemented in a smaller firm that nonetheless manages large funds.

The point is to show versatility: DORA applies broadly, but context matters. Each case study ends with "lessons learned":

- For BigBank: Even large, resource-rich firms have blind spots; DORA helped address complexity and complacency.
- For FinStart: Even small players can punch above their weight in resilience by being proactive and smart, not just throwing money at the problem.

These narratives help readers see themselves in the story and gather practical tips relevant to their context. They also keep the book from being abstract by giving concrete outcomes (like "after doing X, company Y was able to handle Z situation effectively").

Chapter 17: Operational Resilience and Business Continuity

This chapter explores the relationship between DORA's digital operational resilience focus and the traditional field of Business Continuity Management (BCM). Many organizations have long had business continuity and disaster recovery plans (BCP/DR) as part of their risk management, and here we show how DORA elevates, strengthens, and integrates with those practices.

BCM Recap: Business Continuity Management is about keeping critical business processes running through disruptions, and Disaster Recovery (DR) typically refers to the IT side of restoring systems after a disaster. Before DORA, banks and others likely had BCPs (for scenarios like natural disasters, power outages, etc.) and did DR exercises (like data center failovers). Regulators (like banking supervisors) already expected continuity plans, but DORA makes them more rigorous and specifically digital-focused.

DORA's impact on BCM:

- DORA essentially codifies BCM for the digital era. Where BCM might have been a separate silo, DORA integrates it: requiring not just any plan, but one that includes ICT-specific scenarios and is tested. For example, DORA says you need an ICT-focused business continuity policy and recovery plans. This means traditional BCP documents must be reviewed and likely updated to cover cyber incidents, data corruption, etc., not just building fires or floods.
- We point out that DORA uses terms like " ICT business continuity policy" and "ICT response and recovery plans", which align with BCM but with a tech twist. Essentially, your existing BCP/DR documentation should be checked

against DORA's requirements. Are all critical functions identified? Did you include scenarios of cyberattack or tech failure? Do plans include communication strategies for tech incidents (which in the past might have focused on physical disasters)?

Resilience vs. Recovery:

Operational resilience is a broader concept than traditional continuity. BCM often aimed for recovering within an acceptable time (Recovery Time Objective, RTO). DORA's emphasis is on resilience, meaning not just recovering but *maintaining* critical operations continuously if possible, or minimizing downtime dramatically. We explain that DORA pushes firms to think in terms of impact tolerance (a term from UK regulation like resilience): e.g., define how long you can afford for online banking to be down (say 2 hours) and ensure plans meet that. If previously the DR plan had 24 hours RTO for some services, DORA might force a review - is that too long for an "operationally resilient" expectation? Possibly yes for critical ones.

Embedding digital resilience into BCM:

We advise that companies integrate their DORA program with their BCM program:

- Use the same governance where possible (maybe the Business Continuity Committee and the DORA committee share info or merge).
- Update Business Impact Analyses (BIA) to include digital dependencies. For instance, a BIA for payments process should explicitly note reliance on IT systems X, Y, Z and third parties, and potential cyber threats to them.
- Revise continuity plans to include response to cyber incidents (e.g., ransomware scenario: beyond IT fix, how do you continue serving customers if systems are locked? Maybe use manual workarounds or alternate channels temporarily).

- Ensure backup arrangements consider data integrity (backups safe from cyber compromise) as well as availability.

Testing synergy:

Historically, BCM would involve drills like fire drills or DR switch-over tests. DORA requires similar tests. The difference is perhaps increased frequency or scope. We encourage to combine them: when doing a disaster recovery test (like switching to a secondary data center), also simulate a cyberattack scenario to test decision-making and comms. Or vice versa, incorporate continuity fallback steps in a TLPT scenario (e.g., if red team "takes out" System A, do teams know the manual workaround?).

Elevating BCM to the board:

Many times, BCM was considered an operational level issue. DORA's board engagement requirement means business continuity gets board attention too. Board members will ask "Are we operationally resilient?" not just "do we have a dusty BCP binder?" This elevation can mean more funding and support for continuity initiatives that may have been under-resourced earlier.

Supply chain continuity:

Business continuity traditionally considered loss of a building or IT. DORA adds focus on third-party failure. So now continuity planning includes "what if our cloud provider goes down?" - do we have an alternate or a way to manage? The chapter suggests enhancing BCM by adding contingency plans for key vendors (like have a plan if Vendor A isn't available - can you temporarily switch to manual ops or an alternative?).

Crisis Management alignment:

BCM often includes a crisis management team for big incidents. That aligns with DORA's incident management. We discuss ensuring the Crisis Management Plan covers digital crises and ties into the incident response plan. Possibly mention that roles like a crisis communication lead, etc., should coordinate with the ICT incident manager.

Regulatory expectations pre- and post-DORA:

Before DORA, there were guidelines (e.g., the European Central Bank had some guidance, national regulators had continuity requirements). DORA unifies and raises the bar. For instance, previously a small firm might not have been explicitly required to do a sophisticated cyber drill; now under DORA even medium ones should at least test. We may reference that "the Central Bank of Ireland's 2023 guidelines on resilience were a precursor, but DORA is more ambitious in both scope and timeline."

Benefits of strengthened BCM via DORA:

We highlight that companies which truly integrate DORA and BCM will likely handle disruptions better. Perhaps recount a quick scenario: *Two banks face the same issue of a major telecom outage. Bank A had practiced such scenario as part of DORA/BCM alignment, so they swiftly switch to backup communications and continue most services. Bank B had a plan on paper but never tested - chaos ensues, customers can't reach services. Outcome: Bank A's reputation intact, Bank B faces angry customers and scrutiny.*

This drives home that all this planning and testing pays off beyond compliance.

Understanding Synthetic Full Backup Systems

Such systems can enable great resilience and RTO (Recovery Time to Operation) of almost 0 if hardware can be available and immediately reconfigured.

Synthetic full backup starts with an initial complete backup of all data and then uses incremental backups (capturing only changes) to synthesize a new, complete, up-to-date backup at regular intervals or after each modification. Unlike traditional full backups, which require copying all data repeatedly, synthetic full backups combine the initial full backup with incremental changes in the backup repository, creating a new full backup without impacting production systems. This approach minimizes RTO by enabling near-instant recovery, as the latest synthetic full backup is always ready to restore without the need to wait for the full recopy of the data because it is already complete and ready to use.

Key Features:

- Initial Full Backup: Captures all real data (e.g., databases, applications, configurations).
- Incremental Updates: Tracks changes (e.g., file modifications, database updates) in real-time or at scheduled intervals.
- Synthetic Consolidation: Merges incremental changes into a new full backup in the background, ensuring a complete, up-to-date copy without re-copying unchanged data.
- Near-Zero RTO: Allows instant or near-instant restoration, as the latest synthetic full backup is immediately accessible.
- Examples: Solutions like Veeam Backup & Replication, Cohesity, Rubrik, and Commvault support synthetic full backups with advanced features like instant recovery and immutable storage.

Advantages of Synthetic Full Backup Systems Under DORA

These advantages focus on DORA's requirements (Articles 11-12, 24-26) and your goal of near-zero RTO, tailored for financial entities.

Near-Zero RTO for DORA Compliance:

- DORA Requirement: Article 12 mandates backup and recovery procedures that ensure restoration within a two-hour window, minimizing downtime and maintaining business continuity.
- Advantage: Synthetic full backups enable instant or near-instant recovery (e.g., via Veeam's Instant VM Recovery), achieving an RTO of practically zero. This exceeds DORA's

requirements, ensuring financial entities can resume operations immediately after an ICT incident (e.g., ransomware, hardware failure).

- Example: A bank using Rubrik's synthetic full backups can restore a payment processing system in seconds, meeting DORA's stringent recovery timelines.

1. **Enhanced TLPT Readiness (Pillar 3)**:
    - DORA Requirement: Pillar 3 (Articles 24-26) requires advanced testing, including TLPT, to simulate real-world cyber threats and validate recovery capabilities.
    - Advantage: Synthetic full backups provide a complete, up-to-date dataset for TLPT, allowing financial entities to test recovery under realistic attack scenarios (e.g., data encryption, system compromise) without impacting live systems. The near-zero RTO ensures test results reflect production-ready recovery speeds.
2. **Data Security and Integrity**:
    - DORA Requirement: Article 11 requires backups to be segregated, protected from unauthorized access, and compliant with data integrity and confidentiality standards.
    - Advantage: Synthetic full backups can be stored in immutable, air-gapped repositories (e.g., Cohesity's DataLock, NetApp SnapLock), preventing tampering or reinfection during recovery. This aligns with DORA's security mandates and supports testing in isolated environments.
    - Example: A financial entity can store synthetic full backups in a secure cloud, ensuring compliance with

DORA's segregation requirements during TLPT.

3. **Efficiency and Scalability**:
    - DORA Requirement: DORA encourages cost-effective and scalable solutions for continuous compliance (Article 12).
    - Advantage: Synthetic full backups reduce storage and processing demands by consolidating incremental changes without redundant full backups. They scale efficiently for large datasets (e.g., banking systems), minimizing costs and supporting frequent TLPT cycles.
    - Example: Commvault's synthetic full backups reduce backup windows by 50%, allowing a firm to test recovery daily without operational disruption.
4. **Support for Third-Party Risk Management (Pillar 4)**:
    - DORA Requirement: Pillar 4 mandates managing risks from third-party ICT providers (e.g., cloud backup vendors).
    - Advantage: Synthetic full backups can be managed independently or with third-party providers (e.g., AWS with Veeam), reducing reliance on sensitive data sharing. Immutable backups mitigate risks of third-party breaches, aligning with DORA's oversight requirements.
5. **Continuous Resilience Improvement**:
    - DORA Requirement: Pillar 3 emphasizes iterative testing to improve resilience over time.
    - Advantage: Synthetic full backups enable frequent, low-impact testing due to their efficiency and instant recovery capabilities. This supports DORA's requirement for ongoing resilience enhancements, as firms can refine recovery processes after each TLPT.

6. **Regulatory Trust and Competitive Edge**:
    - DORA Requirement: Proactive compliance builds trust with regulators and customers, offering a competitive advantage.
    - Advantage: Implementing synthetic full backups demonstrates a commitment to cutting-edge resilience, exceeding DORA's minimum requirements. The near-zero RTO enhances customer confidence in uninterrupted services.

DORA doesn't replace BCM - it turbocharges it. For readers who have BCM programs, use DORA to update and deepen them. For those who didn't give BCM much thought, DORA essentially forces you to. The result is a more robust organization that can weather not just IT issues but any operational shock better.

The key message is continuity = resilience. DORA ensures that continuity plans aren't just for show but actively practiced and covering modern threats. So rather than see DORA as separate from BCM, see it as the next evolution of it.

We might end with a quote or principle: "Operational resilience is the outcome of good business continuity planning,resilient systems by design plus strong security and risk management - DORA brings these together."

Chapter 18: The Consequences of Inaction

This chapter serves as a cautionary discussion of what can happen if organizations do not take DORA (and operational resilience in general) seriously. It outlines the risks and penalties of non-compliance and, more broadly, the fallout from failing to improve resilience.

Regulatory Penalties:

We outline the formal consequences defined by DORA:

- Fines: As mentioned earlier, regulators (ESAs or NCAs) can impose significant fines for non-compliance - up to 2% of global annual turnover for firms for critical third-party providers, fines can be even higher (up to €5 million or more). These are comparable to major data protection or NIS2 fines, signaling how serious the EU is. We might remind that NIS2 fines go to €10M for big ones, whereas DORA's are slightly lower in % but still very impactful.
- Sanctions on individuals: DORA allows fines on responsible individuals up to €1,000,000(meaning top managers could personally be fined, which is rare in regulations but underlines accountability).
- Other measures: Regulators could issue public reprimands (naming and shaming in press releases), impose restrictions (e.g., limit a bank's operations until issues are fixed), or in severe cases, ultimately impact licensing. Imagine a scenario: if a firm persistently fails to address glaring resilience issues, a regulator might say "no expansion or new products until you comply" or even force changes in management.

Legal Liability:

Beyond regulatory fines, consider legal actions. If a major incident occurs due to negligence in resilience, customers or counterparties might sue. For example, if a bank's systems collapse and clients suffer losses because the bank ignored known IT risks, those clients might pursue damages. Or investors might file lawsuits if they think the management breached fiduciary duty by not safeguarding the bank's operations.

Operational and Financial Damage:

Inaction on resilience can lead to actual incidents that cost a lot:

- Downtime costs: Every hour a payment system is down can mean millions in lost transactions or penalties (e.g., failing to settle trades could incur costs).
- Recovery costs: Fixing a big incident after the fact can be far more expensive than prevention. Ransomware example: pay ransom (if one chooses, which is also problematic), rebuild systems, hire consultants, etc., can run into tens of millions, not to mention regulatory fines for the incident itself if data is lost (GDPR fines) or services disrupted (DORA fines possibly).
- Insurance implications: Cyber insurers may ask about DORA compliance now; if you are non-compliant, maybe claims get harder or premiums go up.

Reputational Damage:

We stress that trust is key in finance. A major IT meltdown or breach will make headlines (customers unable to access accounts, personal data stolen). If it's revealed that it happened because the firm skimped on resilience efforts (e.g., didn't patch systems, ignored warnings), the public fallout is severe. Customers will flee if they feel a bank is not reliable or safe. Once reputation is damaged, it's hard to regain, which translates to long-term financial loss and strategic setbacks. We might reference an anecdote: *There have been instances where banks with prolonged IT failures lost customers to competitors, and their brand took a hit on trust rankings.* Or mention how a big data breach can cause lasting brand damage (like cases of credit card breaches causing customer churn).

Regulatory scrutiny and intervention:

If you're not taking action, expect more visits from regulators. They might put you under "special measures", require frequent updates, or even in extreme cases, regulators can require a bank to hold more capital due to operational risk (like if they think your ops risk is high, they might use Basel rules to increase capital requirements as a buffer). This indirectly hurts your bottom line.

Loss of competitive edge:

In the modern market, being digitally resilient can be a selling point. The chapter posits that companies ignoring it will fall behind. They might face more outages while competitors who invested stay up - guess who customers prefer? Also, partnerships in finance (like big corporates choosing a bank) may evaluate resilience. If you can't demonstrate it, you might lose business contracts. Particularly, if a firm aims to partner with big players or government, they may be asked about compliance (like RFPs could require "compliance with DORA or similar").

Systemic risk contribution:

For bigger institutions, if they ignore resilience and something catastrophic occurs, they could threaten broader financial stability. Regulators could then intervene very sternly. For example, if a big payment system is lax and gets taken down, it's not just that firm - it can hit the economy. The responsible firm could then face not just fines but structural changes (regulators might force them to split critical functions or hand over operations to a more stable entity).

Cultural impact:

We could note internally, if leadership doesn't enforce resilience, front-line IT staff or risk managers might get demotivated or leave, knowing the house is built on sand. Good talent might not want to work at a place known for cutting corners on security - and losing key staff further weakens resilience.

We might illustrate with a hypothetical "Tale of Two Banks":

- Bank Secure invested in resilience, and when a large regional power outage occurred, they kept services running on backups. Customers praised their reliability.
- Bank Neglect ignored needed upgrades; when a similar outage hit, they had no working generator due to poor maintenance - a multi-day outage ensued. Media criticized their poor planning, regulators launched an investigation, customers left in droves, and eventually the CEO resigned under pressure.

Regulatory case examples:

If any actual enforcement happened by 2025 in related areas (like maybe under NIS1 or national guidelines), we can mention: e.g., *UK's regulator fined a bank millions for IT failures in 2018 (TSB incident) due to poor operational risk management.* Or *the Dutch central bank issued orders to improve after some bank's outage.* These show regulators mean business.

Conclusion of this chapter:

It basically warns: *Inaction is not an option.* Not doing anything about DORA and resilience has dire consequences: if the regulations don't get you, reality will. The cost of compliance is dwarfed by the potential cost of a major operational failure. And beyond cost, there's the trust and future of the business on the line. We encourage the mindset that investing in resilience is far smarter than facing these aftermaths.

We might end the chapter on a motivational note: Instead of fearing the consequences, use them as impetus. The knowledge that fines and disasters await inaction should galvanize action today. A quote like "An ounce of prevention is worth a pound of cure" fits well here - implementing resilience now (prevention) avoids paying the heavy price of incidents later (cure).

Chapter 19: Building a Resilient Future

In this chapter, we look beyond mere compliance to emphasize the positive outcomes and strategic advantages of embracing operational resilience through DORA. It's a forward-looking wrap-up that reinforces the value of all the efforts discussed and inspires the reader to see DORA as more than just a checkbox exercise.

From Checklist to Culture:

We reiterate that while we've been through requirements and steps, the goal is to make resilience part of the organization's DNA on all systems and make sure data and services consistency and consistent recovery and availability on all systems to be part of a generalized approach and efficiently managed. DORA is a catalyst, but the change must also be cultural: everyone values and works towards resilience continuously.

Trust and Confidence:

Building strong operational resilience instills trust among all stakeholders:

- **Customers** gain confidence that they can rely on your services anytime. In finance, trust is everything; if customers trust that their bank will be secure and available, they stay loyal and even recommend it.
- **Partners and counterparties** feel secure doing business with you. If you're a bank that other banks rely on for payments or an insurer that banks partner with, showing resilience makes you a preferred partner (they know you won't be the weak link).
- **Investors** and shareholders appreciate reduced risk. A resilient company is less likely to have shocking losses or brand damage, making it a stable investment. One could

argue as well that companies that manage operational risk well might get better credit ratings or investment ratings.

Competitive Advantage:

We highlight that compliance can turn into a competitive advantage. For instance, if your bank's app is known to rarely, if ever, go down, whereas a competitor's app has frequent glitches, you can market that reliability. Or when onboarding corporate clients, you can explicitly mention your robust resilience program (without too much jargon) to set them at ease. Some might fear that resilience is internal and invisible, but good marketing can subtly emphasize it (e.g., "99.99% uptime last year" as a bragging right, which is the result of resilience efforts).

Innovation and Resilience:

Often there's a false dichotomy that focusing on risk slows innovation. We argue the opposite: knowing you have a resilient foundation frees you to innovate more confidently. If you have strong incident response and backups, you might be bolder in adopting new tech because you have safety nets. Also, part of DORA is testing new things in safe ways (like TLPT pushes you to think like an attacker, which can spur innovative defenses). When resilience is integrated, digital transformation projects will include robust design (security and continuity by design), resulting in stronger new products.

Long-term Sustainability:

Operational resilience is about long-term survival and success. History has examples of companies that didn't survive big shocks. We can reference how resilience is akin to resilience in nature: those who adapt and harden themselves against stress survive and thrive. Financial institutions face more digital threats, so resilience is a must for sustainability. DORA essentially ensures the sector's stability in the face of 21st-century challenges (cyber threats, complex IT failures).

Beyond DORA - holistic resilience:

We acknowledge DORA is one piece of the puzzle. A resilient future likely involves:

- Addressing emerging risks (AI and quantum computing come, new threats will appear - a resilient org is one that constantly updates its risk management).
- Possibly integrating with other frameworks (GDPR, NIS2 we discussed, but also upcoming ones like the AI Act or Climate-related risks for physical resilience - e.g. climate change causing more physical disruptions).
- Community and systemic approaches: the more each firm is resilient, the more the whole financial system is. So, by doing your part, you contribute to a stronger economy that benefits everyone, including your own business (less chance of a systemic crash or panic caused by one player's failure).

This book is part of a series "Made Easy" book series on major regulations and may be used in conjunction with other books in the same series.

We can mention that just as DORA enhances digital resilience, other regulations like GDPR and NIS2 (and maybe future ones like the AI Act or Digital Services Act) each strengthen aspects of the trust framework in the digital economy. A truly forward-looking organization stays on top of all these and finds synergies. The book series ("Compliance Made Easy") will continue to guide on those, highlighting that a resilient future is also about privacy (GDPR) and broader cybersecurity (NIS2). So, the journey doesn't end with DORA; it's a continuous improvement across multiple fronts.

Emphasize the mindset: Instead of seeing regulatory compliance as a burden, see it as building a better business. The Digital Operational Resilience Act, with all its detailed requirements, basically pushes companies to be the best version of themselves in terms of stability and security. It's an opportunity to upgrade your operations comprehensively.

We could use a brief metaphor or quote: e.g., *"Resilience is the capacity to bounce back - and bounce forward - in the face of adversity."* With DORA, organizations will bounce back faster from incidents and may even bounce forward (improve) after them, constantly becoming stronger. Even better, if you can make the system so resilient as to withstand major incidents easily with no disruptions even better. Think Netflix "Chaos Monkeys" that disconnect physically servers while watching to make sure other Video streaming servers take over without the user even noticing and delay or problems while watching a film, or even beter, Netflix "Chaos Guerillas" that disconnect complete racks or even data centers randomly and expecting no interruption whatsever.

Ensure that as a leader or professional, you champion resilience in your organization. Encourage readers to take pride in becoming resilience advocates. Because in the end, it's not just about avoiding fines - it's about protecting your customers, your employees, and the integrity of the financial system.

DORA might be challenging, but through it, you essentially build a shield and a compass: a shield against threats and a compass pointing to best practices. As the digital landscape evolves, this foundation will help navigate whatever comes next.

By building a resilient future, you're not just complying with regulation - you're safeguarding the trust, stability, and success of your organization for years to come. That encapsulates the ultimate vision of DORA and our book.

Chapter 20: Conclusion & Next Steps

In this concluding section, we tie everything together and provide final thoughts. We briefly summarize how DORA has guided us to fortify all aspects of digital operations in financial services - from governance and risk management to incident response, testing, third-party oversight, and information sharing. The conclusion reiterates that operational resilience is a journey, not a destination. DORA's framework is now in place, but keeping resilient will be an ongoing effort that evolves with new threats and technologies.

We encourage readers to take what they've learned and act on it. If you're a decision-maker, empower your teams and allocate resources to resilience. If you're an implementer or specialist, engage colleagues and management to drive these initiatives. Use this book as a roadmap but continue learning and adapting.

We also remind the reader that this book is part of a larger series aimed at demystifying complex regulations. Today it's DORA; tomorrow it might be GDPR Made Simple (personal data protection) or NIS2 Made Simple (wider cybersecurity compliance). We suggest that building a comprehensive compliance and resilience strategy across all these areas will create synergies and make your organization robust and trusted in all dimensions.

As next steps, we propose:

- Conduct an internal debrief or workshop with your team using this book's structure to assess readiness.
- Engage with industry peers, share best practices, and learn collectively (echoing the info-sharing spirit).
- Keep an eye on updates: technical standards, guidance from ESAs, etc., will refine obligations - treat this as a living process.

Finally, we end on a motivational note: Embracing DORA is more than just meeting a law - it's joining a movement towards a safer, more reliable financial system in the digital age. Your efforts contribute to that greater good, and in return, you secure your organization's place in a future where trust and resilience are paramount.

DORA Made Simple - Sources & Resources

Source / Website	Description	Relevance to DORA	URL
EUR-Lex – DORA Regulation (EU 2022/ 2554)	Official EU legal text of the Digital Operational Resilience Act.	Primary law and baseline for all requirements.	https://eur-lex.europa.eu/ eli/reg/2022/2554
EIOPA – Digital Operational Resilience Act	European Insurance and Occupational Pensions Authority resources on DORA.	Provides context, Q&A, and supervisory perspective.	https://www.eiopa.europa.eu
ESMA (European Securities and Markets Authority)	DORA implementation in securities markets.	Regulatory guidance for financial markets participants.	https://www.esma.europa.eu
EBA (European Banking Authority)	Guidelines on ICT risk and DORA compliance.	Specific supervisory guidelines for banks and payment providers.	https://www.eba.europa.eu
NIS2 Directive (EU 2022/ 2555)	Updated Network & Information Security Directive.	DORA cross-references NIS2 for incident reporting and resilience.	https://eur-lex.europa.eu/ eli/dir/2022/2555
GDPR (EU 2016/679)	EU General Data Protection Regulation.	Overlaps with DORA on breach notification and governance.	https://eur-lex.europa.eu/ eli/reg/2016/679
CER Directive (EU 2022/ 2557)	Directive on Critical Entities Resilience.	Complements DORA by addressing non-financial critical infrastructures.	https://eur-lex.europa.eu/ eli/dir/2022/2557
FS-ISAC (Financial Services Information Sharing and Analysis Center)	Global threat intelligence sharing for financial institutions.	Referenced in case studies (BigBank, FinStart) for information sharing.	https://www.fsisac.com
TLPT (Threat-Led Penetration Testing) – TIBER-EU	Framework for red-team testing mandated under DORA.	Guidance for implementing resilience testing.	https://www.ecb.europa.eu /paym/cyber-resilience/ tiber-eu

ISO 27001 / ISO 22301 Standards	Information Security & Business Continuity standards.	Frameworks supporting compliance with DORA resilience requirements.	https://www.iso.org
NIST Cybersecurity Framework	U.S. framework for cybersecurity and risk management.	Referenced as a benchmark for ICT risk management.	https://www.nist.gov/cyberframework
Cloud Service Providers (AWS, Azure, GCP)	Third-party ICT providers.	Highlighted in case studies for contractual risk, SLA, and resilience obligations.	https://aws.amazon.com/ https://azure.microsoft.com /https://cloud.google.com

Understanding EU regulation shouldn't be complicated - and that's exactly what this book delivers. EU Directive DORA Made Simple breaks down the complex Digital Operational Resilience Act (DORA) into clear language, real-world examples, and practical steps. Whether you're in compliance, risk management, cybersecurity, IT operations, or executive leadership, this book helps you grasp the "why," "what," and "how" of DORA without the legal jargon.

This guide provides essential insights on how DORA impacts financial institutions, ICT third-party providers, and regulatory frameworks across the EU. You'll learn about risk management obligations, ICT incident reporting, digital resilience testing, governance expectations, and third-party risk requirements - all explained in a straightforward, actionable format. Each chapter is designed to help you build internal awareness, drive alignment, and begin the journey to compliance.

This book is part of the acclaimed "Regulatory Essentials Made Simple" series, created to empower professionals with clear, structured understanding of complex EU directives such as DORA, NIS2, GDPR, and more. Whether you are a newcomer or a seasoned professional looking for clarity, this series is your go-to resource for mastering compliance in the digital age - one directive at a time.

Willy DANENBERG is a seasoned consultant, author, and international speaker specializing in digital compliance, cybersecurity, and regulatory transformation across Europe. With years of hands-on experience guiding major institutions through complex frameworks like DORA, GDPR, and NIS2, he is known for making dense regulations accessible, actionable, and engaging. His writing combines professional rigor with clarity, helping readers turn legal mandates into strategic advantage.

ISBN 979-890030635-3

www.ingramcontent.com/pod-product-compliance
Lightning Source LLC
LaVergne TN
LVHW090421210926
848480LV00002B/647
* 9 7 9 8 2 3 1 6 1 3 9 9 1 *